Build Self-Love
& Break All Limits

Learn to set boundaries, unlock your purpose, and build a positive mindset to create the life you deserve.

Talia James

Contents:

Introduction

A Journey of Self-Love, Boundaries, and Empowerment

Have you ever found yourself standing in front of the mirror, asking, "Who am I really?" Wondering if you're enough or if you'll ever get things right? Trust me, I've been there. More times than I care to admit. I was once a woman who didn't fully love herself. I didn't understand my worth. I had no clue how to set boundaries, how to honor my emotions, or how to prioritize my own happiness. But here's the thing—I was also a woman who was hungry for change. Hungry to break free from the self-doubt, the negative self-talk, and the endless cycle of seeking validation from others.

But here's what I learned: the real change comes when you decide to love yourself first. Not just love yourself on the surface, but deeply, authentically, and unapologetically. It's when you stop pouring from an empty cup and start filling yourself up with what you truly need. When I took that leap into self-love, everything shifted. It wasn't an instant transformation. It was a journey—one that required time, introspection, and a whole lot of patience with myself. But let me tell you, it was worth every step.

I started showing up for myself with love and respect, and everything around me started to change. I became more confident, more resilient, and at peace with who I was. I stopped giving away pieces of myself to others in an attempt to be liked or accepted. Instead, I nurtured the parts of me that had been buried beneath layers of fear, self-doubt, and insecurity. And in that process, I discovered my strength, my power, and my potential.

This journey isn't just about me. It's about you—the woman reading this book, looking for a way to embrace yourself fully, to love yourself fiercely, and to break free from the limiting beliefs holding you back from the life you deserve. I didn't write this book to tell you my story. I wrote it because I want you to experience the same transformative power that self-love gave me.

How Self-Love Changed My Life: The Benefits I Gained

Before discovering the power of self-love, I was living on autopilot. Stressed, self-critical, and constantly seeking approval from the world around me—whether it was from my relationships, career, or society's standards of success. I wasn't truly living for myself. And let me tell you, that kind of life takes a toll on your mental, emotional, and physical well-being.

When I embraced self-love, everything changed. My mental health improved drastically. I experienced less anxiety, less negative self-talk. Instead of battling myself, I began showing myself compassion. I realized that I didn't have to be perfect to be worthy. This realization was freeing.

I also became more resilient. Life's challenges didn't feel so insurmountable. Instead of spiraling into self-pity, I learned to approach obstacles with a solution-oriented mindset. Problems became opportunities to grow, to learn, and to tap into my true potential.

But perhaps the most profound change was the development of my boundaries. Before, I'd say yes to everything, overextend myself, and end up exhausted, resentful, and burned out. Now, I know how to say no—without guilt. I protect my time, my energy, and my peace. Setting boundaries became an act of self-respect. And in doing so, I've cultivated healthier relationships—not just with others, but with myself.

Self-love also helped me discover my purpose. I stopped living according to other people's expectations and started following my passion, aligning with my values, and contributing to the world in a way that felt authentic to me. That sense of purpose has been one of the most fulfilling parts of my journey.

Lastly, self-love gave me the confidence to pursue my dreams without fear of judgment or failure. I stopped letting perfectionism rule my life. Instead of fearing failure, I saw it as a natural part of growth. I learned to trust myself, take risks, and show up fully, knowing that I had my own back, no matter what.

Why I'm Sharing This Knowledge with You

I'm sharing this knowledge because I want you to know your worth. I want you to feel empowered to live your truth, love yourself unapologetically, and embrace the life you deserve. This book isn't just for me—it's for you. For every woman who has ever doubted her worth, who has neglected her needs, or who has forgotten the power of boundaries. I want this book to be your guide, to help you rediscover your strength, reclaim your happiness, and create a life aligned with your deepest desires.

By the time you finish this book, I hope you'll see yourself as the beautiful, worthy, and capable woman you truly are. I hope you'll feel inspired to put yourself first, set those essential boundaries, and build a life that reflects who you really are no apologies, no compromises.

But most of all, I want you to feel empowered. Empowered to say no when you need to. Empowered to chase your dreams, even when fear tries to hold you back. Empowered to love yourself fiercely, without guilt, shame, or hesitation. Because when you start putting yourself first, everything else falls into place.

Now, it's time for you to claim the life you were always meant to live.

With Love,
Talia James

"You become what you believe."

Oprah Winfrey

What the f* does self-love mean?

Self-Love

Alright, let's set the record straight. Self-love isn't about some mystical vibe where everything is sparkles, glitter, and endless good vibes. In reality, self-love is about treating yourself with the same respect and care you'd give to someone you love deeply. Think about it: how often do we extend kindness, forgiveness, and understanding to others, but hold ourselves to impossible standards? We pick apart our own mistakes, compare ourselves mercilessly to others, and rarely stop to say, "Hey, I'm doing okay."

Real self-love is showing up for yourself like you'd show up for your best friend. Imagine your friend was feeling low or making mistakes—would you tell her she's unworthy or unlovable? Of course not. You'd probably remind her that everyone has bad days, and you'd help her see her strengths again. Self-love is about extending that same empathy inward. It's not about bubble baths and chocolates alone (though those help!). It's about waking up in the morning and deciding to be on your own team, even when it feels like the world isn't.

Humor can actually be a big part of self-love. Why? Because self-love doesn't mean taking everything, especially yourself, so seriously all the time. Laugh at your quirks, accept your flaws, and realize that we're all a little ridiculous sometimes. You can love yourself while still acknowledging that you have things to work on. Self-love is the act of saying, "I'm worthy of love and respect, even as I grow." It's about balance: holding yourself accountable but also forgiving yourself. Imagine giving yourself permission to be human. That's the foundation of true self-love.

Why Self-Love Isn't Selfish

Let's break down the myth that self-love is selfish. We're taught, especially as women, that putting ourselves first means we're ignoring everyone else. But here's the truth: if you're constantly giving away your time, energy, and support without taking time to refill, you're going to hit a wall. Self-love means taking care of your needs so you can genuinely be there for others. Think of it like this: if you're exhausted, you're not helping anyone. Your energy isn't endless, and self-love is about recognizing that.

Imagine you're on a plane, and they tell you to put your oxygen mask on before helping anyone else. Why? Because if you're not breathing, you can't help anyone else. That's self-love in a nutshell. When you prioritize your well-being, you're better equipped to show up for others from a place of wholeness, not obligation. Self-love means recognizing that you deserve to feel fulfilled, to rest, and to set boundaries that protect your energy. When you do that, the love you give to others is genuine, not forced. It's given freely, not from a place of resentment or exhaustion.

Self-love isn't about saying "no" to others all the time—it's about knowing when to say "yes" to yourself. It's about filling your own cup, so when you give to others, it's from a place of abundance, not depletion. There's nothing selfish about valuing your own mental health, your happiness, and your peace of mind. Remember, it's okay to be your own priority. In fact, it's essential.

What Self-Love Isn't

This might be one of the most misunderstood parts of self-love. Let's start by clearing up a big misconception: self-love isn't ego. It's not walking around thinking you're better than anyone else. Self-love is not entitlement. It's not believing that the world owes you something. True self-love is a humble, grounded acceptance of who you are. It's saying, "I'm worthy of respect and kindness, just like anyone else," but not expecting to be treated differently or to receive more than anyone else.

A lot of people confuse self-love with arrogance. They think that if you love yourself, you're full of yourself. But arrogance is rooted in insecurity; it's a shield people use to hide their fears and doubts. Self-love, on the other hand, is a quiet confidence. It's knowing that you have value without needing to prove it to anyone. It's not about boasting or acting superior; it's about holding space for yourself, just as you are, flaws and all.

Self-love also isn't about being selfish. It's not disregarding others' needs. Think of it like building a foundation: if your foundation is strong, you can support others without falling apart. If your foundation is shaky, trying to support everyone else is only going to lead to collapse. Self-love means setting boundaries, not because you don't care about others, but because you care about yourself enough to protect your peace. Boundaries are a form of self-love, and they're essential for healthy relationships.

Why Self-Love is So Important

Self-love isn't just a "nice-to-have"; it's the bedrock of everything in life. When you value yourself, it shows up in every decision you make. In relationships, self-love means you don't settle for people who don't treat you well. You recognize your worth, and that changes the people you attract and the way you allow yourself to be treated. If you're constantly doubting your worth, you're more likely to accept treatment that doesn't honor you.

In your career, self-love means you're more likely to pursue goals that fulfill you, not just the ones that are "safe" or "expected." When you believe in yourself, you're more willing to take risks, to try new things, and to chase your dreams, knowing that you deserve success and happiness. Without self-love, we make choices out of fear, thinking we're not capable of more, that we don't deserve more. Self-love shifts that mindset.

Self-love affects mental health, too. When you're kind to yourself, you're less likely to spiral into self-doubt and self-criticism. You recognize that setbacks and failures don't define you; they're just parts of the journey. Self-love allows you to see your worth beyond your achievements, beyond your mistakes. It's the reminder that, no matter what happens, you're still worthy of compassion.

The Benefits of Cultivating Self-Love

When you start to cultivate self-love, life begins to change.

First, you notice a shift in how you feel about yourself. There's a newfound peace that comes from knowing you're not constantly at war with yourself. Self-love leads to better mental health, less stress, and a greater sense of calm. Instead of feeling like you're constantly "not enough," you begin to see that you're more than enough, just as you are.

Relationships improve, too. Self-love helps you set healthier boundaries, which means you're less likely to tolerate behavior that drains or disrespects you. You attract people who appreciate you, who see your worth, because you see it in yourself. It's like holding a mirror up to the world—when you value yourself, others start to value you too.

Self-love also leads to a confidence that's rooted in truth. This isn't about being cocky; it's about knowing your value. When you truly love yourself, you stop comparing yourself to others because you understand that your path is unique. You realize that you have your own strengths and gifts, and that there's room for everyone to shine.

How Self-Love Can Change Your Life

Self-love can transform your life in ways you might never expect. It can give you the courage to go after your dreams, to leave situations that aren't serving you, and to pursue happiness unapologetically. Self-love isn't a luxury; it's a necessity. When you start to treat yourself with love and respect, you'll find that your whole life begins to align with that energy.

Imagine taking the small, daily steps to show up for yourself.

Choosing to say "no" when you need rest. Giving yourself grace on a hard day. These little acts build a life of self-love, and over time, they create a life that feels fulfilling and true to who you are. Self-love isn't a destination; it's a journey, and every step you take is a testament to your worth.

When you commit to loving yourself, life responds. You start to see more beauty in the world, more possibility, because you're finally looking at life through a lens that honors who you truly are. Self-love is about learning to be on your own side, to trust yourself, and to see your life as something worth investing in. And when you start to live from that place, you'll find that your life changes in ways you never thought possible.

"It is impossible to live without failing at something, unless you live so cautiously that you might as well not have lived at all—in which case, you fail by default."
J.K. Rowling

1. Mastering Self-Love & Owning Your Worth

1.1 Make Yourself a Priority

Define and Respect Your Own Needs

Alright, let's dive right in: if you don't make yourself a priority, who else will? Think about it. Society has conditioned so many of us to feel guilty for putting ourselves first. We're told to take care of everyone around us, to be "selfless" and "giving," and that somehow, asking for what we need or want is "selfish." Well, let's throw that idea out the window, shall we? Making yourself a priority isn't selfish—it's essential.

Imagine if you spent your whole life waiting for permission to take care of yourself. It sounds ridiculous, right? And yet, so many of us live that way. Making yourself a priority means realizing that your needs are valid and worth honoring. Let's break this down in the most straightforward terms, so you can see just how transformative this shift can be.

What Does It Mean to Make Yourself a Priority?

When we talk about "making yourself a priority," we're not talking about ignoring others or shirking responsibilities. We're talking about giving yourself permission to focus on your well-being. It means recognizing that you are just as worthy of time, effort, and care as anyone else in your life. Here's the truth: if you keep putting yourself last, eventually, there's going to be nothing left to give.

Putting yourself first is about understanding and respecting your own needs—both the big, soul-deep ones and the day-to-day basics that keep you grounded.

So, what does that look like? Here's a roadmap to get started.

Identify Your Needs

The first step to making yourself a priority is actually knowing what you need. Sounds simple, but you'd be amazed at how many people struggle with this. We're often so focused on everyone else that we lose touch with our own desires, needs, and even basic preferences. Take some time to really ask yourself: *What do I need?* Your needs can be physical, emotional, mental, or even spiritual. They can be long-term goals or immediate comforts.

Here's how to start:

- *Create a list of your non-negotiables* – the things that keep you feeling like *you*. Think of this as the basics: sleep, good food, movement, a bit of quiet time.
- *Separate what's truly necessary from what's just a "should"* – if you're writing down things that don't actually matter to you but feel like obligations, drop them. This is about what *you* genuinely need, not what society, friends, or family say you should do.
- *Add joy to your needs list* – Needs aren't only about survival; they're also about what makes life feel good. If a walk in the park or a good book keeps you grounded, add it.

Reframe Guilt as a Signal

Let's get real about guilt. Guilt is one of the main reasons we don't put ourselves first. We've been trained to feel guilty anytime we do something "just for us." But here's the thing: guilt is often a learned response, and it doesn't always tell the truth. If you feel guilty for saying no, for taking time off, or for setting boundaries, remind yourself that guilt doesn't mean you're doing something wrong. It just means you're doing something different.

Try this:

- Acknowledge the guilt but don't let it control you. Notice it, name it, and then ask yourself if it's really valid.
- *Flip the script* – every time guilt shows up, remind yourself why you're setting this boundary or making yourself a priority. Let the reason why you're doing it be louder than the guilt.
- *Treat guilt as a reminder of your worth* – if you feel guilty for caring for yourself, use that as a cue to remind yourself that you are deserving of love, care, and respect.

Set Boundaries Like a Pro

Setting boundaries is a game-changer. Boundaries help you carve out space to take care of your needs without burning out. When you set a boundary, you're not being mean; you're simply saying, "This is what I need to be okay." And let's face it—no one else will set these boundaries for you.

We'll dig even deeper into boundaries later in this book, covering how to set them in relationships, at work, and even with yourself. For now, here's how to start:

- *Define your limits* – know where your "enough" is, in time, energy, or emotional effort.
- *Communicate unapologetically* – boundaries aren't about pleasing others; they're about protecting your peace.
- *Hold firm* – people might push back, but standing your ground is necessary.

Practice Daily Self-Compassion

Self-compassion is like a daily vitamin for self-worth. When you're compassionate toward yourself, you're less likely to beat yourself up over mistakes, setbacks, or perceived flaws. Practicing self-compassion means speaking to yourself with kindness and patience. It's one of the most powerful ways to make yourself a priority because it shifts your internal dialogue from criticism to care.

How to practice self-compassion:

- *Check your inner dialogue* – every time you catch yourself being harsh or judgmental, flip the script and try kindness.
- *Treat yourself like a friend* – if your best friend was struggling, you wouldn't tell her she's failing. Why say it to yourself?
- *Forgive your mistakes* – self-compassion means understanding that messing up is part of being human.

Create "Me Time" That Actually Feeds Your Soul

We often think of "me time" as just another item on our to-do list, like squeezing in a quick face mask or scrolling on social media. But real me time should feed your soul. This could be anything that makes you feel recharged and fulfilled.

Here are some ideas for meaningful "me time":

- *Journal your thoughts* – this can help you connect with what you really want and need.
- *Get outside* – nature has a way of grounding us and helping us reconnect with ourselves.
- *Engage in something creative* – whether it's painting, cooking, or dancing, creativity is a powerful way to nurture yourself.

Commit to Regular "Self-Check-Ins"

Life is always shifting, so the things you need might change too. One of the most effective ways to stay connected to yourself is by regularly checking in. Ask yourself how you're feeling, if your needs are being met, and if any changes are needed.

Self-Check-In Prompts:

- How am I feeling right now?
- What do I need more of, and what do I need less of?
- Is there anything I'm doing out of obligation that I can let go of?

Celebrate the Small Wins

When you start making yourself a priority, celebrate it. Every time you choose yourself, it's a victory. It might not feel monumental at first, but every small step adds up. Maybe you said "no" to an extra commitment this week, or you went to bed early instead of pushing yourself to finish that one last task.

Those moments deserve recognition.

Ways to Celebrate:

- Keep a "Wins" journal to track all the little things you've done for yourself.
- Reward yourself with something you love—a cup of coffee, a cozy blanket, a solo date.
- Tell a friend! Sharing your wins can make them feel even more significant.

Making Yourself a Priority Isn't a One-Time Thing—It's a Lifestyle

Ultimately, making yourself a priority isn't a one-off decision. It's a way of life. It's choosing, every day, to honor your needs, respect your limits, and value yourself. When you start treating yourself as a priority, you'll notice a shift in how you feel, how others treat you, and even in the opportunities that come your way. It's not magic, but it's powerful.

And here's the best part: you don't have to wait for anyone else to give you permission to make yourself a priority. You get to decide that you're worth it. So go ahead, set those boundaries, listen to your needs, and remember—you're not just making a choice for today. You're building a life that honors who you are, every single day.

"Self-worth comes from one thing—
thinking that you are worthy."

Oprah Winfrey

1.2 Accept Yourself

Embracing Every Facet of Yourself

Alright, let's get real. When we talk about accepting yourself, we're not talking about some half-hearted, "Yeah, I guess I'm okay." We're talking about radical acceptance. Radical acceptance is the unapologetic embrace of every part of who you are—the parts that shine, the parts that stumble, and the parts you'd rather hide from the world. This is the kind of acceptance that doesn't have a footnote of "when I lose ten pounds" or "once I've accomplished something." It's about saying, "This is me, right here, right now, and I'm done apologizing for it." Radical acceptance is rebellion against the messages you've been fed about what it means to be "good enough" or "worthy." Let's face it: we live in a world that profits from our insecurities. Advertisements, media, social pressures—they all sell us the lie that if we just fix this or change that, then we'll be worthy. Radical acceptance calls that out as the BS it is. It means deciding that you don't have to change to be lovable or valuable. You are enough as you are.

So, how do you begin accepting yourself radically? How do you get to the place where you can look in the mirror, flaws and all, and feel genuinely okay with what you see?

Steps to Radical Acceptance

1. Acknowledge Your "Flaws" Without Apology
2. *Start with a basic truth:* You're not flawed. You're just human. Society likes to label things that make us unique as "flaws" because they don't fit neatly into a one-size-fits-all mold. But who decides what's a flaw? When you stop apologizing for every part of yourself that doesn't fit someone else's idea of "perfect," you begin to reclaim your power.
3. Are you too loud? Maybe for some people. But loud is also bold, confident, and unapologetically you.

- Are you "too emotional"? Good. Emotions are what make us alive, sensitive, connected. Feelings are messy but beautiful, and embracing them is part of radical acceptance.

Look in the mirror and ask yourself, "Who am I apologizing to? And why?" Most of the time, our perceived flaws are what make us unique and extraordinary. You owe nobody an apology for being who you are. When you apologize for being yourself, you hand over control of your worth. Take it back.

Challenge the Concept of "Good" and "Bad" Traits

So many of us categorize our traits as "good" or "bad," "acceptable" or "unacceptable." But this mindset is limiting. You are complex and multi-dimensional. There are parts of you that contradict each other, and that's okay. It's part of the beauty of being human. You can be strong *and* vulnerable, kind *and* assertive, confident *and* insecure. All these qualities coexist within you.

Take the time to explore your personality and habits. Instead of judging them, just notice them. Ask yourself:

1. What do these traits do for me?
2. How do they show up in my life?
3. When are they helpful, and when are they not?

Often, what we consider "bad" traits are just traits that society hasn't learned to value. Some people hate their stubbornness, but it's that same trait that can give them persistence. Radical acceptance means recognizing that no trait makes you inherently "bad." Every part of you serves a purpose.

Give Yourself Permission to Be Imperfect

Listen: *You will never be perfect.* Nobody will. The more you chase perfection, the more disappointed you'll feel because that bar will always be out of reach. When you start giving yourself permission to mess up, you also give yourself permission to be human. Self-acceptance is not about being flawless; it's about embracing your humanness, imperfections and all.

Here's a little exercise:

- Write down a list of times you "failed" or "messed up" in your life.
- Next to each one, write what you learned from it or how it helped you grow.

This exercise reminds you that every slip-up and stumble has been a stepping stone in your journey. You wouldn't be who you are today without these experiences.

Let Go of Perfectionism: Find Freedom in Being Enough

Perfectionism is the voice that says, "You could be a little better." It's the voice that convinces you that if you were just *a little smarter, a little prettier, a little more put-together,* then you'd be worthy. But perfectionism is a toxic illusion—it keeps you locked in a cage, forever chasing something that doesn't even exist.

Here's the raw truth: perfectionism isn't about *being* perfect; it's about *appearing* perfect. It's about trying to meet expectations that you didn't set for yourself in the first place.

How to Release the Grip of Perfectionism

1. *Question Where These Standards Come From*

Take a moment to think about who or what has set the standards you're holding yourself to. Are they even your standards? Did you decide that you need to look a certain way, or did you absorb that from magazines, Instagram, or family expectations? The first step to letting go of perfectionism is realizing that a lot of these standards were never yours to begin with.

- *Ask Yourself:* Who benefits from me believing that I'm not enough? Spoiler alert: It's not you. Perfectionism keeps you dependent on outside validation and approval. Once you let go of these standards, you reclaim the right to set your own.

Aim for Progress, Not Perfection

Growth is what matters, not some fantasy of "arriving" at a perfect version of yourself. Focusing on progress allows you to celebrate the little wins instead of dismissing them because you haven't reached some imagined end goal.

1. Celebrate each step forward, no matter how small.
2. Notice the progress you're making, even if it's just a tiny bit each day.

When you stop expecting yourself to be perfect, you start seeing the beauty in your journey, flaws and all.

Learn to Sit with Discomfort

Perfectionism often thrives because we're uncomfortable with failure or looking less-than-perfect. But radical acceptance means learning to sit with discomfort without trying to fix it. It's about being okay with not having all the answers or having everything put together.

1. Practice sitting with the discomfort of not being perfect. Remind yourself that you are still valuable, worthy, and lovable, even when things don't go as planned.

Embrace the Freedom of Being "Good Enough"

There's a sense of freedom in choosing to be "good enough." Imagine letting yourself be just as you are—right here, right now, with nothing to prove. Being "good enough" doesn't mean you don't have dreams or ambitions; it means you're no longer willing to put your worth on hold until you achieve them. You are worthy today, exactly as you are.

Key Takeaways for Radical Acceptance

- Own Your Uniqueness: Embrace what makes you different. Your quirks are your power.
- Rewrite Your Standards: Drop unrealistic expectations and set standards that serve you.
- Celebrate Progress: Every step forward is worth acknowledging. Perfection isn't the goal; growth is.
- Stay Present: Radical acceptance is about embracing who you are in this moment—not in some hypothetical "better" future.

Radical self-acceptance is your invitation to show up for yourself, as you are, without apology. It's not always easy, but each step toward accepting yourself is a step toward freedom. Freedom from perfectionism, from the need to prove yourself, and from the exhausting idea that you need to be someone else to be worthy. Because you, just as you are, are enough.

"We may encounter many defeats, but
we must not be defeated."
Maya Angelou

1.3 Self-Compassion

Practicing Self-Compassion in Difficult Moments

Let's face it—being kind to yourself isn't as easy as it sounds. In fact, when things go wrong, it's often the hardest thing to do. But that's when it matters most. Self-compassion isn't about coddling yourself or giving up on growth; it's about being there for yourself when the going gets tough, not as a judge but as an ally. In this chapter, we're going to dive deep into why and how you can develop self-compassion, especially during those inevitable rough patches when you most need someone in your corner—and that someone is you.

Why Self-Compassion Matters: More Than a Nice Idea

You might wonder, "Why do I need to be kind to myself when I've messed up? Doesn't that just encourage weakness?" Actually, self-compassion is the opposite of weakness; it's resilience in action. It's a way of anchoring yourself in kindness and acceptance, even when things are messy. Self-compassion is about understanding that you deserve care, not because of what you achieve, but simply because you're human. And if you can't show that kindness to yourself, you end up relying solely on external validation, leaving you vulnerable to life's ups and downs. Self-compassion makes you your own steady support system.

1. *Recognizing Your Own Pain and Validating It*

The first step toward self-compassion is simple but profound: *recognizing* your pain and letting yourself feel it. Sounds basic, right? Yet so many of us shove our pain down or dismiss it, thinking, "Other people have it worse," or, "I shouldn't feel this way." But your pain is valid, no matter how big or small. When you ignore or judge your own feelings, you're effectively saying, "I don't deserve to be cared for." Self-compassion means accepting that your feelings are real and worthy of attention.

Here's an exercise to start:

- Notice and Name Your Feelings
- Whenever you're feeling overwhelmed, anxious, sad, or frustrated, take a moment to acknowledge it. Just say, "I'm feeling [insert feeling]." There's power in naming what you're going through because it allows you to take a compassionate stance, acknowledging that you're having a hard time.
- Give Yourself Permission to Feel

Remind yourself that it's okay to feel this way. You're not weak or broken. You're simply human. Emotions, especially difficult ones, need to be felt and processed to be released. Allow yourself to experience them without judgment.

2. *Silencing the Inner Critic and Replacing It with Self-Kindness*
Let's talk about the inner critic—the voice inside that loves to pop up when things aren't going well. This critic can be brutal, whispering (or yelling) things like, "You're so stupid," "How could you mess this up?" or "You'll never get it right." It's harsh, relentless, and completely unhelpful. Self-compassion starts with actively choosing to silence that critic and replace it with kindness.

- *Challenge Your Inner Critic's Lies*

Your inner critic is an expert at twisting reality to make you feel smaller. Start to notice the patterns in its messages. Is it always telling you that you're "not enough" or "never good at anything"? Once you see these patterns, challenge them. Ask, "Is this really true? Would I say this to a friend?" Chances are, you wouldn't.

- *Replace Criticism with Reassurance*

This is about giving yourself grace. When you make a mistake, instead of saying, "I can't believe I messed that up," try, "Everyone makes mistakes, and this doesn't define me." Imagine the relief and calm that would follow if you gave yourself that small gift of understanding.

3. *Practicing Mindful Self-Compassion*

Mindfulness is the practice of being present with what is, without judgment. When combined with self-compassion, mindfulness can be transformative. It allows you to observe your feelings and experiences with gentle curiosity rather than harsh judgment, creating a safe mental space for yourself.

- *Observe Without Judgment*

When you're going through something difficult, practice observing your thoughts and feelings without reacting to them. Imagine you're watching a movie of your life. Notice how it feels, and let yourself sit with those feelings. This doesn't mean wallowing; it's about giving yourself a moment to just *be* without trying to fix or change anything.

- *Treat Your Thoughts Like Passing Clouds*

Picture each thought as a cloud passing by. You don't need to latch onto it, and you don't need to fight it. Just let it float by. You'll notice that most thoughts are temporary—they come and go. This practice reminds you that even in hard times, your feelings are not permanent. They're a part of your journey, not the whole story.

4. *Speaking to Yourself Like You Would to a Loved One*

This step is at the heart of self-compassion: treating yourself with the same kindness and support that you'd offer a friend. Imagine a dear friend comes to you, brokenhearted, stressed, or disappointed in herself. Would you tell her to "suck it up" or "get over it"?

No, you'd listen, offer a hug, and remind her of her worth. Why not give yourself that same compassion?

- *Create a Script for Self-Compassionate Responses*

When you're struggling, it can be hard to think of supportive things to say to yourself. So, create a script in advance. Write down a few self-compassionate phrases you can use when you're having a tough time. Examples include:

- "I know this is hard, and it's okay to feel this way."
- "Mistakes are part of growth, not a sign of failure."
- "I am worthy of kindness, even when things go wrong."

Keep these phrases on hand for the moments when you need them most.

- *Practice Saying "I'm Here for You" to Yourself*

When you feel alone in your pain, remind yourself that you can be there for you. Even if no one else understands, *you* do. Close your eyes, put a hand on your heart, and say, "I'm here for you." It may feel awkward at first, but this simple practice is a powerful reminder that you are never truly alone.

Self-compassion is about recognizing that you're worthy of kindness and patience, no matter the circumstance. In the end, it's not about avoiding hard times or escaping pain. It's about showing up for yourself, through it all, with open arms and a kind heart. You are your own greatest support system, capable of offering love and understanding even in the darkest moments. Embrace it, practice it, and know that you deserve it—every single day.

"It's never too late to be the person you
were meant to be."
Jane Fonda

1.4: Breaking Free from Limiting Beliefs

What Are Limiting Beliefs and Why Do They Hold Us Back?
Let's get real—limiting beliefs are like mental roadblocks, making life harder, keeping us small, and sabotaging our self-worth. They're those little (or sometimes loud) voices that whisper things like, "You're not smart enough," "You'll never succeed," or "Who do you think you are to even try?" Limiting beliefs are ideas that we've somehow internalized about ourselves, believing them so deeply that they shape our actions, choices, and ultimately, our lives.

Limiting beliefs often come from experiences in childhood, societal expectations, or well-meaning (but misguided) advice from family, friends, or teachers. The problem is, these beliefs don't stay confined to a single area of life—they seep into everything, limiting what we believe is possible for us. The result? We live a life far smaller than the one we're capable of.

Recognizing Your Own Limiting Beliefs
To break free, you first need to know what you're working with. It's time to shine a spotlight on those hidden beliefs that hold you back. Often, they're buried so deep that we operate on autopilot without even realizing they're there.
Try this exercise:

1. Write Down a Goal You Want to Achieve
2. It can be anything: a career change, a fitness goal, or starting a new hobby. Don't overthink it—just write down something meaningful to you.
3. List All the Reasons You Think It Won't Happen

This is where things get interesting. Write down every reason why you think this goal isn't possible for you. It could be doubts like, "I don't have the time," "I'm too old," "I'm not talented enough." Whatever comes to mind, jot it down.

- Notice the Patterns

Look at your list. These reasons are your limiting beliefs in action. Do you notice any themes? Maybe there's a belief that you're "not enough" or that "success is for other people." Identifying these beliefs is the first step to breaking free from them.

Understanding the Origins of Your Limiting Beliefs

Now that you have a list of beliefs, it's time to dig deeper. Most limiting beliefs don't just pop up out of nowhere—they're usually rooted in past experiences, other people's opinions, or societal messages. By understanding where these beliefs came from, you can begin to detach from them, realizing that they aren't facts; they're simply stories you've been told or have told yourself.

Some common sources of limiting beliefs include:

- *Family Expectations:* Growing up, you may have been told to "play it safe" or that "people like us don't do that." These messages can shape your beliefs about what's possible for you.
- *Past Failures:* If you've tried something in the past and it didn't work out, you might've formed the belief that you're "not capable." But failure doesn't define you; it's just a stepping stone on the path to growth.
- *Societal Conditioning:* Society has a way of pushing certain narratives, especially for women. Whether it's about beauty standards, career paths, or relationship roles, these expectations can create limiting beliefs that we unconsciously adopt.

Challenging and Rewriting Your Limiting Beliefs

Here's where we start transforming these beliefs. Challenging limiting beliefs is about questioning their validity, poking holes in them, and ultimately realizing that they're not facts—they're opinions that don't serve you.

To challenge a limiting belief, try asking yourself these questions:

- *"Is this belief absolutely true?"*

Most of the time, the answer will be no. Just because you failed once doesn't mean you'll fail every time. Just because someone said you "couldn't" doesn't mean it's true.

- *"Where did this belief come from?"*

Understanding the origin of the belief can help you see that it's not a universal truth. Maybe someone told you once that you "weren't good at math," but that doesn't mean you can't develop new skills.

- *"What evidence do I have that contradicts this belief?"*

If you believe you're "not good enough," think about times when you *have* succeeded, times when you've been strong, capable, or resilient. Collecting evidence against your limiting beliefs is a powerful way to weaken their grip.

Replacing Limiting Beliefs with Empowering Affirmations

Once you've identified and challenged your limiting beliefs, it's time to replace them with new, empowering beliefs that reflect your true potential. Affirmations are a tool for doing just that. They're positive statements that counteract your negative self-talk, helping to rewire your brain to see possibilities instead of limitations.

Here's how to create powerful affirmations to replace your limiting beliefs:

1. *Make Them Personal and Specific*

Your affirmation should feel true to you. If you're working to overcome a belief that you're "not capable," try something like, "I am fully capable of achieving my goals and worthy of success."

2. Use Present Tense
Phrase your affirmation in the present tense, as if it's already true. Instead of saying, "I will be confident," say, "I am confident."

3. Believe in What You're Saying
It's okay if it feels awkward at first; that's normal. But try to feel the truth in your words, even if it's just a spark. Over time, that spark will grow, and you'll start to believe it.

4. Repeat, Repeat, Repeat
Repetition is key. Write your affirmations down, say them out loud, and remind yourself of them daily. The more you reinforce these positive beliefs, the stronger they become.

Practicing Self-Compassion Along the Journey
Breaking free from limiting beliefs isn't easy, and it doesn't happen overnight. It's a journey that requires patience, persistence, and a lot of self-compassion. There will be times when those old beliefs try to creep back in, but that's okay. What matters is that you keep going, keep challenging, and keep choosing to believe in yourself.

Remember, self-compassion isn't about "letting yourself off the hook." It's about understanding that change takes time and that you deserve grace along the way.
Here are some self-compassionate reminders to carry with you:

- *"Growth isn't linear, and that's okay."*
Progress isn't always a straight line, and setbacks are part of the journey.

- *"I am worthy of love and respect, just as I am."*

Your worth isn't tied to what you achieve or how fast you grow.

- *"It's okay to start again as many times as I need."*

Each day is a new chance to rewrite your beliefs and build a life that reflects your true potential.

Embracing Your New Beliefs

As you practice these affirmations and start to shift your mindset, you'll begin to see changes. Maybe you'll notice yourself taking risks you once avoided, speaking up more confidently, or simply feeling a little lighter. These are signs that your new beliefs are taking root, and they deserve to be celebrated.

Breaking free from limiting beliefs is one of the most empowering things you can do for yourself. It's a gift that keeps giving, helping you to create a life that reflects your worth, courage, and potential. So, celebrate each step forward, no matter how small. You're rewriting your story, one belief at a time.

"You have to be unique, and different,
and shine in your own way."
Lady Gaga

1.5 Building Self-Confidence

Recognizing and Valuing Every Achievement

One of the most underrated paths to real self-confidence is appreciating every step of your journey—each small victory, every milestone, and even the moments that might seem insignificant at first. Every achievement, no matter its size, is a stepping stone toward something greater.

So, how do you get into the habit of truly recognizing and valuing your achievements?

- *Start a "Daily Wins" Journal:* Dedicate a journal solely to recording your accomplishments. Don't overthink it; if you did it and it helped you move forward, it counts. Writing things down helps reinforce a sense of achievement, making it real and tangible.

- *Celebrate Both Internal and External Achievements:* Remember, not all victories are about outward results. Some days, just getting out of bed or dealing calmly with a difficult situation is a huge win. For example, if you stayed grounded in a stressful moment or managed to finish a challenging task, those are internal achievements that deserve recognition.

- *Reflect on Past Achievements Regularly:* Take time once a week to go through your journal or list of accomplishments. Remind yourself of your journey, the obstacles you overcame, and the resilience you showed. This reflection is like refueling your confidence tank with proof of your own capability.

Celebrating What Makes You, You

Comparison is a confidence killer. The truth is, there's no

one else on this planet who has exactly what you have to offer. Embracing your uniqueness is about seeing the value in your quirks, experiences, and strengths and recognizing that they are what make you irreplaceable.

- *Create a List of "Superpowers":* Write down everything that makes you uniquely powerful, whether it's your resilience, your creativity, your kindness, or even your humor. When you identify these strengths, you're giving yourself permission to be proud of who you are. This list can be a personal reminder to stop striving to be like anyone else because you already have so much to offer.

- *Affirm Your Worth Daily:* Pick a few affirmations that resonate with you, like "I am valuable for who I am, not just what I achieve" or "I am proud of my unique perspective." Place these affirmations somewhere visible and make a habit of saying them to yourself each day. Over time, these affirmations shift from words into beliefs.

- *Reframe Your "Weaknesses":* Society tends to label certain traits as "weaknesses," but many of these can actually be strengths when viewed differently. For instance, sensitivity can mean you're in tune with others' emotions, or being detail-oriented could be an asset in fields that require precision. Embracing the full spectrum of who you are, including the so-called "weaknesses," gives you a more balanced and confident sense of self.

Setting Realistic Goals to Boost Confidence: The Power of Small Steps

Setting goals is a fantastic way to build confidence, but it's essential to start where you are and set realistic, achievable steps. This isn't about playing it safe; it's about setting yourself up for consistent, sustainable growth.

- *Create SMART Goals:* Use the SMART method (Specific, Measurable, Achievable, Relevant, Time-bound) to set each goal. For example, instead of saying, "I want to be more organized," try "I will organize my workspace for 15 minutes each day for one week." This structure makes it easier to track progress, and each day you achieve it, you reinforce your capability.

- *Make a Weekly Action Plan:* Set one goal each week that you're excited about achieving. Break it down into tiny steps, and check off each one as you go. Maybe you want to try a new skill, like cooking a new recipe or speaking up in a meeting. With every step, you're building a sense of achievement, and confidence grows with every small action completed.

- *Celebrate Progress Over Perfection:* Real confidence is less about nailing everything on the first try and more about showing up, learning, and growing along the way. Give yourself credit for effort and progress instead of expecting perfection. At the end of the week, review what you accomplished and recognize every step forward, no matter how small.

Building Resilience Through Self-Compassion: A Lifelong Confidence Booster

Self-compassion is your secret weapon for lasting confidence. Why? Because confidence isn't about avoiding mistakes or never failing. It's about bouncing back. When you show yourself kindness and understanding, especially in moments of difficulty, you're reinforcing an unshakeable belief in your own worth.

- *Speak to Yourself Like a Best Friend:* Imagine your best friend just went through a tough time. How would you comfort them? What would you say? Now, say those words to yourself. When things go wrong, say, "It's okay. I'm allowed to feel this way, and I can get through it."

- *Practice Self-Compassionate Touch:* Physical gestures like placing a hand over your heart or giving yourself a gentle hug can help soothe you during stressful moments. It may sound a bit unconventional, but research shows that self-compassionate touch activates the parasympathetic nervous system, helping to calm you down and reduce stress.

- *Reflect on Moments of Resilience:* Think back to a time when you overcame a setback. What helped you get through it? Reflecting on past resilience reminds you of your own strength and builds confidence in your ability to handle challenges in the future.

Practicing Positive Self-Talk: The Ultimate Confidence Builder
Your mind is like a loudspeaker, constantly feeding you messages about who you are and what you can (or can't) do. Practicing positive self-talk rewires your brain to believe in your potential and recognize your worth. It's a game-changer for confidence.

- *Challenge Negative Thoughts:* When a negative thought pops up, don't let it go unchecked. Ask yourself, "Is this thought true?" or "What evidence do I have to support this?" Often, you'll realize that these thoughts are assumptions or beliefs that don't hold up to scrutiny.

- *Use the Power of "Yet":* When you find yourself thinking, "I can't do this," add "yet" at the end. "I can't do this...yet." It reframes the thought from a fixed limitation to a future possibility.

- *Create a Positive Mantra:* A mantra like "I am capable, and I am growing every day" can be a powerful confidence booster. Repeating a mantra when you're feeling doubtful serves as a mental reset, reminding you of your strength.

Act the Way You Want to Feel

Confidence isn't just a mental state; it's also physical. The way you hold yourself can directly impact how you feel. Adopting powerful, open body language sends signals to your brain that you are confident, capable, and ready for anything.

- *Power Posing:* Before a big event or when you're feeling uncertain, try a "power pose." Stand tall, place your hands on your hips or raise your arms in a V-shape. Holding a power pose for two minutes has been shown to reduce cortisol (the stress hormone) and increase feelings of confidence.

- *Mindful Breathing:* Practice breathing deeply and slowly, especially in situations where you feel nervous. Deep breathing calms the nervous system, helping you feel grounded and in control. When you're relaxed, you're more likely to appear and feel confident.

- *Mirror Exercises:* Stand in front of the mirror each morning, make eye contact with yourself, and affirm your worth. It might feel awkward at first, but looking yourself in the eyes and saying, "I am proud of you," can have a powerful impact on your self-image and confidence.

Surrounding Yourself with Positivity

The people around you play a massive role in your self-confidence. Surrounding yourself with positive, supportive individuals who believe in you creates an environment where confidence can thrive.

- *Identify Your "Confidence Circle":* Think of the people in your life who genuinely lift you up. These are the friends, family members, or mentors who see your potential, even when you don't. Make an effort to spend more time with these people.
- *Limit Exposure to Negative Influences:* You don't need to cut people out of your life, but you can set boundaries with individuals who tend to bring you down. Be mindful of how certain people make you feel, and prioritize relationships that leave you feeling valued and uplifted.
- *Seek Out Positive Communities:* Find groups or communities that share your interests or values. This could be anything from a hobby group to a professional network. Being part of a community that respects and supports you reinforces your confidence and provides a safe space to grow.

Confidence doesn't appear overnight, but with consistent, intentional actions, it grows into an unstoppable force within you. Every time you choose to believe in yourself, celebrate your wins, and show up with kindness and resilience, you're building a foundation for lasting self-confidence. Remember, you are worthy, capable, and equipped with everything you need to succeed.

"Owning our story and loving ourselves through that process is the bravest thing that we'll ever do."

Brene Brown

2. Claiming the Life You Were Meant to Live

2.1 Exploring Your Passions

Owning Your Happiness

Let's be real. Life can often feel like one big list of "shoulds." You should find a stable job. You should settle down. You should prioritize everyone else first. But the truth is, following these shoulds can sometimes leave us empty and unfulfilled. Finding your passions and giving them room to breathe in your life is how you claim that life you've always wanted. It's the real you, before anyone told you who you had to be. This chapter is about digging out those hidden or neglected passions and making space for them to shine.

Why Exploring Your Passions Matters

Think of passions as the secret ingredients in a recipe. You might not need them to get by in life, but once you add them, everything is richer, fuller, and more satisfying. Passions feed your soul; they give you energy, joy, and purpose. Here's why they matter so much:

- *They make life exciting:* Without passions, days blend together. Passions pull you forward, giving you something to look forward to.
- *They remind you of your uniqueness:* Everyone has their own set of passions that makes them who they are. Embracing them helps you see your own worth.
- *They help you grow:* Exploring what you love pushes you outside your comfort zone, sparking growth, creativity, and self-discovery.

So, stop waiting for permission, stop putting yourself last, and let's jump into finding those passions that make you feel alive

Reflecting on the Activities That Bring You Satisfaction

This might sound obvious, but most of us rarely stop to actually reflect on what we love to do. Let's dive deeper into understanding your happiness.

The 'Joy Audit' Exercise

This exercise is about revisiting the best moments of your life and figuring out what they have in common. Here's how to do it:

- *List Five Moments of Pure Joy:* Close your eyes, think back to times when you felt like you were glowing from the inside out. Write these moments down.
- *Examples:* The time you organized a family gathering and saw everyone laughing, or that solo hike where you felt one with nature.

- *Analyze Your List:* Now, look at each moment and dig into the *why. Reflection Prompts:*
1. "What was it about this moment that made me feel fulfilled?"
2. "Was I alone or with people? Was I creating, teaching, organizing, or exploring?"
3. "Did I feel proud, calm, confident, or energized?"

- This isn't about being productive. It's about feeling alive. As you answer these questions, you'll start seeing patterns emerge. Maybe it's creativity, leadership, peace, or learning. Whatever it is, these moments are clues to what truly fills you up.

Exercises for Identifying Your Talents and Natural Interests

Your talents aren't just skills—they're gifts that can guide you toward your passions. And don't worry; if you don't feel like you have any obvious "talents," it might just be that you haven't recognized them yet.

Talent Inventory

Talent isn't always flashy; sometimes, it's that quiet ease you feel with certain activities. Here's a process to uncover those natural strengths:

- *List Five Things You Can Do Effortlessly:* Don't overthink this. Write down things you're comfortable with and that maybe others have noticed too.
- Examples: You might be a natural at organizing events, comforting people, or thinking up creative solutions to problems.
- *Pinpoint Your Unique Strengths:* Now, think about times when people have praised you or leaned on you for something.
- Reflection Prompt: "What do others say I'm good at, even if I think it's no big deal?" Sometimes, others can see talents in us that we overlook.
- *Consider How You Use These Talents in Daily Life:* Do you find yourself using your talents in specific ways, even if it's just in small moments? This reflection can help you think of ways to bring more of these talents into your day-to-day.

Interest Exploration

Interest is the spark that keeps your attention. It's what keeps you reading, watching, or thinking about something long after others might lose interest.

- *Write Down Five Topics You're Fascinated By:* Don't worry if they don't seem connected or "useful." Just write down five topics or activities you'd lose track of time doing.
- *Examples:* Maybe you could spend hours reading about astronomy, watching food documentaries, or learning about historical figures. Whatever it is, it's yours.
- *Notice How These Interests Make You Feel:* Interests are markers of potential passions. They represent the things that capture your curiosity and enthusiasm. Just because you're not "good" at something doesn't mean it can't be a passion.

Rediscovering Forgotten Passions

Let's talk about those passions you used to have, before life got in the way. This section is about finding what might have been pushed to the side but still holds a piece of you.

Returning to Childhood Dreams
When you were a kid, you had no concept of limitations. Your childhood dreams were pure, unfiltered expressions of joy. Often, they can guide you back to your authentic self.
Exercise: Childhood Passion Discovery

Step 1: Write down three things you loved doing as a kid. Don't censor yourself.

Step 2: Ask yourself why you stopped. Was it time? Fear? Society telling you it wasn't "practical"?

Step 3: Imagine ways to bring a version of that passion back into your adult life.

Example: Maybe you loved painting as a kid, but life got busy. Can you dedicate just one hour a week to picking it back up? Or if you loved animals, could you volunteer at a shelter once a month? Sometimes, we don't outgrow passions; we simply set them aside. This exercise helps you reconnect with those abandoned interests.

Reclaiming "Guilty Pleasures" Without Guilt

Society has a way of making us feel like some activities are "guilty pleasures." Let's ditch that. If something brings you joy, then it's worthy of your time.

Reflection Prompt: "What activities do I love but rarely do because they don't feel 'useful'?"
Write these down, and beside each one, write, "This brings me joy, and that's enough." Give yourself permission to indulge.

Facing Fears and Challenges in Pursuing Passions

Every passion comes with a little fear. That's normal. Sometimes it's the fear of failure, judgment, or even success. Here's how to get past it.

Conquering Self-Doubt

Self-doubt is passion's biggest enemy. But when you talk back to it, you take away its power.

- *Exercise: Flip the Script*
- *Write down all the reasons you're afraid to pursue your passions.*
- *For each reason, write a positive counterstatement. Imagine you're talking to a close friend who needs encouragement.*

Tips to Deepen and Sustain Your Passion Journey

- *Keep a Passion Journal: Document moments that bring you joy, ideas, and small wins. This journal is a reminder that your passions are part of you, and you're investing in yourself every time you explore them.*
- *Connect with Others Who Share Your Passion: When you surround yourself with people who understand your interests, your enthusiasm grows. Find groups, both in-person and online, to support and inspire you.*
- *Set Boundaries Around Your Passion Time: Life will always be busy, but claiming time for yourself is non-negotiable. Treat it as sacred.*

"Don't look for approval from others. Do what you know is right for you."

Tina Fey

2.2 Understanding Your Core Values: The Core of Your Identity

Let's start at the very beginning: what exactly are core values? These values aren't just "things you believe." They're foundational principles that form the backbone of who you are and who you're meant to be. They are the essence of what drives you forward, fuels your passions, and shapes your unique outlook on life. Understanding these values is like finding the key to your most authentic self, an unfiltered version of you that's free from societal expectations and pressures.

Core values are those deep-seated beliefs that have been quietly guiding you all along, even when you weren't fully aware of them. Maybe they come from life lessons, childhood influences, personal experiences, or even the pain of past mistakes. When you identify and truly understand them, you unlock a sense of clarity that makes decision-making feel a whole lot easier.

Why Defining Your Values Matters

Imagine trying to build a house without any blueprints or planning. You could gather all the materials and tools, but without a foundation and structure, the whole thing would fall apart. Living without defined values is a bit like that. Your values provide structure and guidance; they're your moral compass, your map for navigating through life's toughest challenges.

Benefits of Defining Your Values

1. *Gives You a Clear Direction* – When you know your values, you know exactly where you stand and what matters to you most.
2. *Builds Inner Confidence* – Aligning your actions with your values strengthens your sense of self, making you more confident in your choices.
3. *Enhances Personal Satisfaction* – Living by your values

- *brings fulfillment.* You're no longer chasing after things that don't actually resonate with you.
- *Strengthens Resilience* – When you stand by your values, you can handle challenges with a sense of peace, knowing that you're living authentically.

Discovering Your Core Values

Now, let's make this practical. Here's an exercise designed to help you identify your values. Remember, there's no right or wrong here. This is your journey.

- *Reflect on Meaningful Moments*

Think about five pivotal moments in your life. These can be accomplishments, challenges you've overcome, or simple experiences that left a deep impact. Describe each moment in detail—where you were, who was there, how you felt, and why it mattered.

- *Identify the Underlying Values*

Look closely at these moments and ask yourself: "What values were at play?" For example, if a moment was meaningful because it involved helping someone in need, then perhaps "compassion" or "service" is a core value for you.

- *Choose Your Top Values*

Try narrowing down your list to around five or six values. Be specific, and don't settle for general values unless they really resonate. "Love" can be narrowed down to "self-love" or "unconditional love," for example.

- *Create Personal Statements for Each Value*

For each core value, write a statement that explains why it matters to you. It doesn't have to be long, just honest. For example, if "honesty" is a value, your statement might be: "Honesty keeps me aligned with myself and the people I care about. I'd rather be upfront than pretend to be someone I'm not."

What It Feels Like to Honor Your Core Values

Once you've defined your values, the next step is living in alignment with them. Living in alignment means that every action, big or small, respects these values. It means you're honoring who you are in everything you do, from the way you interact with others to the goals you set for yourself. Here's the magic of alignment—it feels damn good. Imagine feeling a sense of peace, knowing you're living in line with what truly matters to you. That's the kind of satisfaction that's worth more than anything else.

Signs You're in Alignment:

Increased Self-Respect – When you honor your values, you respect yourself on a whole new level. You're standing up for what you believe in.

Inner Calm and Confidence – There's a distinct peace that comes from knowing you're living by your values. Decisions feel easier because they're based on principles you trust.

Authentic Joy – This is joy that comes from within, untainted by the need for outside validation. You're not trying to impress anyone; you're simply being you.

Aligning Your Daily Life with Your Core Values

It's one thing to identify your values, but it's another to live them out day by day. Here's an exercise to help bridge that gap:

Take Stock of Your Current Life Choices

Grab a piece of paper and write down a few key areas of your life: work, relationships, hobbies, and health. Under each category, ask yourself if your current actions reflect your core values. Be brutally honest. If you value "growth," are you actively pursuing learning opportunities? If you value "authenticity," are you showing up as your true self in your relationships?

List Out Changes to Better Reflect Your Values
Under each category, note any adjustments you can make to align with your values. Don't feel pressured to overhaul everything at once. Start with small steps. If "well-being" is a value, perhaps it's committing to a daily walk or prioritizing a good night's sleep.

Set a Weekly Check-In
Consistency is key, so create a time each week to check in on your alignment. Ask yourself: "Am I honoring my values?" Celebrate the ways you're succeeding, and consider how you might shift any areas that feel off.

Examples of Value-Driven Choices
- If "freedom" is a core value, you might prioritize work flexibility over a high-paying job.
- If "community" is essential, you may invest more time in friendships or volunteer work.
- If "growth" is at the top of your list, you might set aside time each day for reading or personal development activities.

Embracing the Power of Core Values in Times of Challenge
Living by your values isn't always easy, especially when the going gets tough. But here's the thing—your values are *most powerful* during difficult times. They become your anchor, keeping you grounded and steady when everything else feels chaotic. Think of your values as a lighthouse, guiding you back to what's essential when you feel lost.

How Values Help You Stay Resilient
1. *They Give You Purpose* – When challenges arise, values provide a sense of purpose that's bigger than any temporary setback.
2. *They Offer a Clear Path Forward* – Decisions, even tough ones, become easier when they're based on values. You know what to do because you know what matters.

3. They Remind You of Who You Are – Your values serve as a constant reminder of your strength, integrity, and capability.

Reflection: Handling Difficult Situations Through Values
The next time you face a tough situation, try using your values as a decision-making tool. Ask yourself, "What choice aligns best with my values?" This reflection can reveal a solution that feels both courageous and true to who you are.

The Lasting Impact of Values

Here's a thought: by living in alignment with your core values, you're not just creating a meaningful life for yourself—you're building a legacy. Every action, every choice, and every interaction you have leaves a mark. When you live by your values, you inspire those around you to do the same. This is about more than just personal satisfaction; it's about contributing to the world in a way that's meaningful and impactful.

How Values Influence Your Legacy

- *They Inspire Others* – When people see you living authentically, it gives them permission to do the same. They see the courage and freedom that comes with honoring your truth.

- *They Shape How You're Remembered* – Think about the kind of impact you want to leave behind. Living by your values creates a legacy of integrity, compassion, and authenticity.

- *They Empower Future Generations* – The more you embody your values, the more you create a ripple effect that influences others. You're showing what it means to live a life that's true to oneself.

"When you learn to love yourself, you can begin to love others."

Alicia Keys

2.3 Recognizing Your Unique Contribution

Embracing Your Unique Path

Recognizing your unique contribution isn't about anyone else. It's about looking in the mirror and seeing that every aspect of your life—your strengths, struggles, quirks, and even the mistakes you've made—forms a complex, rich picture of who you are. When you stop looking outward and start exploring your inner world, you uncover what makes you powerful, resilient, and deeply valuable.

This exploration is about claiming your life experiences as part of what makes you whole. You're not a work-in-progress or waiting to become something "better." You're already a complete person with gifts and perspectives that only you possess. Understanding this is about giving yourself permission to feel worthy, proud, and damn good about everything you bring to your own life.

Mining Your Life for Meaning: Understanding Your Story

Think about the experiences that have shaped you the most. Maybe some of them were painful, some triumphant, and some simply quiet moments of realization. Each of these events is a piece of your personal puzzle. They're not just memories; they're clues about who you are.

Your past experiences, especially the hardest ones, have built up reserves of strength, wisdom, and endurance inside you. Take a moment to let that sink in: everything you've been through, survived, and thrived despite, has made you who you are today. Knowing this is empowering because it shows that you have what it takes to navigate whatever comes next.

Reclaiming Your Story

To recognize your unique contribution to your own life, start by exploring the experiences that have shaped you:

List Pivotal Experiences
Write down moments that stand out—big or small. Look for times you felt stretched, changed, or awakened.

Ask Yourself What You Gained
Reflect on each experience and ask: What did I learn about myself here? How did I grow? What strengths or insights did I take away?

Celebrate Your Resilience
Take a moment to appreciate the skills, strengths, and resilience these moments brought to your life. By recognizing what you gained, you're reclaiming these experiences as a testament to your strength and growth.

Afterward, look over your notes. These aren't just memories or "life lessons"—they're the essence of your contribution to your own life journey. Knowing what you've overcome, you start to see how capable, resourceful, and valuable you are.

Honoring What Matters Most to You
Recognizing your unique contribution is also about understanding what really matters to you. When you start aligning your life with these core values, you start to feel a deeper sense of purpose—not because of what you're doing for others, but because you're finally living in a way that feels right for you.

Your values are personal; they're the things that make you feel alive, grounded, and like the truest version of yourself. Living in alignment with these values means making choices, big or small, that honor what matters most to you. It's a way of making sure that every day, you're nurturing and respecting yourself.

Defining Your Unique Contribution to Yourself
This exercise will help you put into words the unique

contribution you bring to your own life:

- *Identify Core Values*

Reflect on what really matters to you. Is it growth, authenticity, compassion, freedom? Write down a few that resonate deeply.

- *Create a Personal Mission Statement*

Using your core values, craft a statement that captures what you want to bring to your life. For example: "I value growth, resilience, and joy, and my unique contribution is to create a life that reflects these every day."

- *Visualize Living in Alignment*

Take a moment to picture yourself living in alignment with your values. How does it feel? Imagine this as your daily reality—a life that feels right, whole, and fulfilling because it's built on what truly matters to you.

- *List Small Actions to Honor This*

Bullet out some small, actionable steps you can take to live in alignment with your mission. These can be anything from setting boundaries, pursuing hobbies, dedicating time to self-reflection, or simply allowing yourself rest. By taking small steps to honor your values, you're making a daily commitment to yourself.

Finding Purpose in Your Own Journey

Recognizing your unique contribution is an ongoing journey, not a final destination. You're constantly evolving, learning, and changing, and that means your unique gifts and values will shift as well. This is about creating a life that honors who you are at every stage. When you focus on nurturing your own growth and happiness, you naturally start living with purpose.

Your purpose isn't a grand, singular goal—it's found in every moment you choose to live in a way that feels right for you. It's found in each day you prioritize self-compassion, each time you

make a decision that aligns with your values, and every moment
you let yourself simply be, without judgment.

This isn't about striving or becoming someone different; it's
about realizing that you already have everything you need to live
a fulfilling, meaningful life. Recognizing your unique
contribution means seeing yourself as whole, valuable, and
worthy, just as you are.

"No one can make you feel inferior
without your consent."
Eleanor Roosevelt

2.4 Embracing Your Journey

Why the Process Is the Real Goal
Society has trained us to believe that success is a finish line—that one day, after we've hustled and "fixed" every part of ourselves, we'll finally cross that line and be worthy. We're conditioned to think that when we have the career, the partner, the perfectly balanced life, then—then—we'll be happy. But the truth is, that line keeps moving. Every time you reach one goal, there's another goal, and then another.

So, what if success isn't the end of the race but the ability to live, love, and grow along the way? Success, when you think about it, is more about resilience than results, more about learning and showing up than any single achievement.

Finding Joy in the In-Between
Think of the happiest memories you have. Are they monumental moments like graduations, promotions, or finally getting that dream job? Or are they the little, everyday moments—the laughter with a friend, the quiet early morning coffee, the small act of kindness that caught you by surprise?

There's a certain kind of magic in these small moments. They're the in-between spaces, the ones we often overlook because they don't look like traditional "achievements." But if you start to pay attention, you'll realize that life is mostly made up of these in-betweens. And when you learn to find joy in them, life itself becomes more fulfilling, even without the big "wins."

Imagine if, instead of racing to the next milestone, you could pause and savor where you are. Those quiet, beautiful moments are like little notes in the song of your life. Each one has a melody, a lesson, and a feeling that no one else will ever experience in exactly the same way. By appreciating these moments, you're teaching yourself that every day holds something of value—that your journey itself is worthy of love.

Practicing Presence to Savor the Now

Start Each Day with Intention
- As soon as you wake up, take a moment to set an intention for your day. It could be as simple as "I will notice the beauty around me" or "I will find one thing to appreciate about myself today." This helps you anchor in the present.

Pause for Gratitude Moments
- Throughout the day, take intentional pauses. Notice something around you that brings you joy or peace, whether it's the sunlight filtering through a window or the warmth of your favorite tea. Take a deep breath and allow yourself to fully experience it.

Close Your Day with Reflection
- Before bed, think about the small moments that brought you happiness or peace. Write them down, or simply replay them in your mind. By consciously reflecting on these experiences, you're building a habit of seeing value in the everyday.

Each of these steps reinforces the idea that your life isn't happening "out there" in the future—it's happening right here, right now. And by honoring the present, you're giving yourself permission to enjoy the journey as it unfolds.

Learning from Where You've Been

A significant part of appreciating the journey is learning to embrace every version of yourself. So often, we judge ourselves for past mistakes, wondering why we weren't stronger, smarter, or more prepared. But here's a radical thought: every past version of you was doing the best she could with what she had at the time. She was navigating life with the tools, knowledge, and strength she had then—and that deserves respect.

Every experience you've been through has shaped you. The

heartbreaks, the missed opportunities, the dreams that didn't come true—they've all contributed to the woman you are today. Learning to honor those parts of your journey is essential for self-love because it means you're accepting every part of yourself, not just the shiny, "successful" parts.

Turning "What Ifs" into "What's Next"

Regret can be a huge barrier to appreciating the journey. It keeps us focused on the past, on what could have been, instead of what is. But regret isn't necessarily bad—it's a sign that you're reflecting, learning, and growing. The trick is to not let it consume you. Instead of seeing past choices as mistakes, try seeing them as teachers. Every "wrong" choice was simply a step that led you to where you are now.

Imagine reframing your regrets this way: instead of thinking, "I wish I had done things differently," ask, "What did that experience teach me, and how can I apply it now?" This shift allows you to take control of your narrative, to see yourself not as a victim of your past but as a student of your own life.

Transforming Regret into Growth

- *Identify a Regret*

Think of a past choice you regret. It could be a relationship, a career choice, or even something you said in a heated moment.

- *Write Down the Lesson*

Ask yourself what this experience taught you. What did it reveal about your needs, values, or boundaries? What would you do differently if faced with a similar situation?

- *Release It with Gratitude*

Consciously let go of any lingering resentment or guilt. Thank that past version of yourself for the growth she facilitated. Remember, every version of you brought you one step closer to who you are today.

This exercise helps you make peace with your past, allowing you to move forward with a sense of freedom. Instead of dragging around the weight of regret, you're transforming it into wisdom, creating a mindset that's open to the present and ready for the future.

Understanding Growth as a Nonlinear Path

We often think of growth as a straight line—a constant progression where each step takes us closer to becoming our "best selves." But the truth is, growth is anything but linear. It's full of ups and downs, moments of clarity followed by moments of confusion, two steps forward and one step back. Sometimes it even feels like we're stuck or moving backward. But remember, this is all part of the journey.

Growth is like a dance. Sometimes you're moving forward, sometimes you're spinning in circles, and sometimes you're standing still. But every movement, every pause, and every misstep is part of the dance. The key is to trust that each phase of growth has something valuable to offer, even if you can't see it yet.

By embracing the nonlinear nature of growth, you're freeing yourself from the pressure to "always be progressing." You're allowing yourself to ebb and flow with life, to honor the times when you need rest just as much as the times when you're in full momentum.

Reflecting on Personal Milestones: Small Victories Add Up

One of the best ways to appreciate your journey is to celebrate your personal milestones. And no, I don't mean only the big, flashy ones. I'm talking about the small victories, the quiet wins, the moments when you chose yourself, even if no one else noticed.

Celebrating your progress means acknowledging the steps you're taking every day to become a better version of yourself. Maybe it's the morning you got out of bed when everything in you wanted to hide under the covers, or the time you held back tears and chose compassion instead of self-criticism. These are victories worth honoring because they're the building blocks of self-love.

Creating a Milestone Journal

- *List Recent "Wins"*

Take out your journal and write down at least five moments in the past month that made you feel proud. They can be as small as choosing to eat a nourishing meal, speaking up in a meeting, or setting a personal boundary.

- *Write the Impact*

Next to each win, write down why it mattered to you. What did this action say about your journey? How did it reflect the person you're becoming?

- *Create a Milestone Collection*

Keep adding to this journal regularly. Every time you experience a small victory, write it down. Over time, you'll have a collection of milestones that remind you of your growth, your resilience, and your commitment to yourself.

Building a Relationship with Yourself through the Journey

Ultimately, appreciating your journey is about building a loving, respectful relationship with yourself. It's about seeing yourself not as a project to be completed but as a complex, ever-evolving masterpiece. You're not here to "fix" yourself; you're here to discover, embrace, and celebrate all that you are.

This is your life, and every moment—every victory, every setback, every quiet day and every loud, exhilarating experience—is part of the story you're creating. When you learn to appreciate the journey, you're learning to love yourself, exactly as you are, in every phase, in every chapter.

So, here's to the journey. Here's to the messy, beautiful, unpredictable path that's uniquely yours. You are enough, right here, right now, every step of the way.

"You are the sum of what you believe. It doesn't matter if it's good or bad, but what you think of yourself is what you become."

Shonda Rhimes

2.5 Overcoming Purpose-Related Fears

Let's talk about change. It's that uncomfortable, anxiety-triggering, nerve-wracking idea that keeps us up at night, even though we know—we know—that it's inevitable. Change is the silent passenger of every decision, every step forward, and every new chapter we turn in life. Yet, it's one of the most intimidating parts of discovering our purpose because, let's face it, the unknown can feel like stepping off a cliff in the dark.

Why is change so damn scary? Because it's unpredictable, because we're creatures of habit, and because (let's be real) we like control. We love knowing what's next, and our brains are practically wired to resist anything that shakes up our routines or the safety nets we've so carefully constructed. But here's the twist: purpose—your unique, powerful reason for being here—lives just beyond those comfort zones. So, to find it, you've got to make friends with change and walk hand-in-hand with uncertainty. No, it's not easy, but it's also not impossible.

Understanding Fear of Change

So, what exactly are we afraid of when it comes to change? Let's break it down. The fear of change usually stems from a few key insecurities:

- *Fear of Failure*

What if I mess this up? What if the new direction I take turns out to be a total disaster? We've all been there, but remember that failure is often just a stepping stone toward success.

- *Fear of Judgment*

When we make a big life change, the people around us might not understand. And let's be real, the idea of judgment—whether from family, friends, or society—can make change feel even more intimidating.

- Fear of Losing Control

This one's a classic. Change disrupts our routines, our expectations, and often, our sense of who we are. And because of that, we feel out of control.

- Fear of Losing Stability

We like the known, even if it's not perfect. Change can feel like we're jeopardizing the things that make us feel secure, like our finances, our relationships, and our sense of identity.

Learning to Navigate the Unknown

When we chase our purpose, uncertainty becomes a constant companion. So, how do we make peace with it?

- *Accepting That Uncertainty Is Normal*

The first step is simple: remind yourself that uncertainty is not a sign of weakness, lack of preparation, or inadequacy. It's normal. *Everyone* who has ever achieved something meaningful has faced it.

- *Shifting Your Perspective on Uncertainty*

Rather than viewing the unknown as something to fear, try to see it as an open canvas. Uncertainty means possibility. It's a reminder that your life is a work in progress, open to whatever extraordinary paths you're brave enough to explore.

- *Redefining What Stability Really Means*

Stability isn't about clinging to the same routine for 50 years. Real stability comes from your own inner resilience, from knowing that no matter what, you can adapt, grow, and keep moving forward. In other words, stability isn't about never changing; it's about feeling solid in your own ability to handle whatever comes.

Embracing Uncertainty

Try this:

Step 1: Write down one big change or unknown that you're currently facing in your life.

Step 2: Next to it, list three possible outcomes. Don't limit yourself to just the negatives; include positives, too. This will help you see that uncertainty isn't just a doorway to failure—it's also a doorway to something amazing.

Step 3: For each outcome, write down one thing you could do to handle it. This practice helps you feel more in control and reminds you that no matter what happens, you're capable of handling it.

One of the most important things to remember as you step into the unknown is that the journey of personal growth is inseparable from the pursuit of purpose. Growth is not some side effect of finding your path; it *is* the path.

So, what does embracing growth actually look like?

Understanding Growth as a Continuous Journey

Sometimes, we think of growth as a linear process—as if we start here and end there, checking off boxes along the way. But real growth is more like a spiral. It circles around, sometimes bringing you back to familiar fears or challenges, but each time, you're a little wiser, a little stronger. And every time you loop back, you get a chance to confront an old fear from a new perspective. Growth is messy, uncomfortable, and often downright inconvenient, but it's also *worth it.*

Growth also means being open to change within yourself. That might mean re-evaluating beliefs you've held for years, embracing new perspectives, and sometimes, letting go of parts

*of yourself that no longer serve you. Growth is about expanding
into the fullest version of yourself, even if that means breaking free
of the familiar.*

Learning to Love Your Evolving Self

*One of the hardest parts of growth is learning to love each new
version of yourself. We often cling to our past selves because
they're familiar, comfortable, and known. But remember, every
version of you has been a stepping stone toward your true purpose.
Embrace the woman you're becoming, flaws and all, because she's
exactly who you need to be for the journey ahead.*

Practicing Self-Acceptance in Growth

- *Reflect on Past Growth*

Think of a moment in the past where you experienced significant
personal growth. Write down what you learned and how that
growth positively impacted your life.

- *Accept the Current Version of Yourself*

Take a moment to appreciate who you are right now. Even if
you don't feel "complete" or "there" yet, acknowledge that this
version of you is doing her best.

1. *Envision Your Future Self*

Imagine yourself five or ten years from now, after more growth
and change. Visualize her strength, wisdom, and the peace she
carries. Keep her in mind as a reminder that growth is always
worth the effort.

Letting Go of "Perfection" in the Pursuit of Purpose

Growth is not about becoming perfect. It's about becoming
whole. The journey toward purpose isn't about "fixing" yourself
or erasing your flaws. It's about uncovering your true self,
embracing both your light and your shadows, and realizing that
every part of you—yes, even the messy parts—has something

valuable to contribute.

When you stop chasing perfection and start embracing your whole self, you begin to feel more at ease with change. You realize that you don't need to be flawless to be worthy of purpose, joy, or love. You just need to be willing to show up, imperfectly and wholeheartedly, for the journey.

Bringing It All Together

The journey to your purpose is going to ask a lot from you. It's going to ask you to face fears, embrace uncertainty, and grow in ways you never imagined. But in doing so, it will also give you everything you need to live a life that feels meaningful and true. Let's be real, this journey isn't for the faint of heart. But remember, you have everything within you to handle it—all the courage, all the wisdom, all the grit. Each step you take, no matter how scary or uncertain, brings you closer to a life that feels genuinely yours.

So, let go of the need to have it all figured out. Embrace change, embrace growth, and, most importantly, embrace the woman you're becoming. She's worth it. And so are you.

"We do not need magic to transform
our world. We carry all the power we
need inside ourselves already."

J.K. Rowling

3. Setting Boundaries & Ditching the Drama

3.1 Identifying Your Personal Boundaries

Let's Talk Boundaries: Why They Matter

When it comes to personal boundaries, you might think of a fence or a line drawn in the sand. But boundaries are more than that—they're the lines we draw to protect our energy, peace, and sense of self. They define what's okay for us and what's not, creating a safe space where we can actually thrive.

And here's the truth: everyone needs boundaries, even the most giving, loving, selfless people. Without them, we end up feeling overwhelmed, resentful, or even a little lost, as if we're living someone else's life instead of our own. But the best part? Once you start setting boundaries, you're not only showing the world that you value yourself, you're also creating the groundwork for healthier, more respectful relationships.

So, let's dive into what these boundaries actually are and why honoring them is one of the most powerful acts of self-love you can ever commit to.

Physical Boundaries

Physical boundaries are probably the easiest to recognize. Think about your personal bubble—the distance you feel comfortable keeping between yourself and others. We all have different levels of comfort here, and there's no right or wrong. For some, hugs are a natural hello; for others, a handshake might feel too close for comfort. Knowing where you stand with physical boundaries is about understanding your comfort zone and honoring your right to say "no."

Maybe you've been in a situation where someone moved in too close, or maybe you felt pressure to hug a family member or friend, even when it didn't feel right. It's in these small moments where we can start to recognize our own boundaries and how often we might push them aside to avoid "being rude" or "making things awkward."

Take a minute to think back on a time when someone was in your space, and you felt uncomfortable. How did you react? Did you step back or find a polite way to move away, or did you freeze and allow the interaction because you didn't want to "make it a big deal"? Recognizing these moments can help you tune into your own physical boundaries and start setting new standards for your comfort.

Your Right to Space
Physical boundaries are your body's way of saying, "This is my space, and I decide who gets to enter it." Don't feel bad about enforcing this. It's a simple but powerful statement of self-respect. The next time you're in an uncomfortable situation, remember: it's okay to say, "Actually, I'm not a hugger," or even to take a step back if someone's crowding you.

Emotional Boundaries: Protecting Your Heart

Emotional boundaries are more complex. They're the limits you set to protect your feelings and mental well-being. Have you ever shared something personal only to have someone dismiss your feelings or try to "fix" the problem without really listening? Or maybe someone unloaded their troubles on you without considering whether you had the emotional energy to take it on. Emotional boundaries help you decide how much of yourself you're willing to share, and with whom.

Think of emotional boundaries as a shield around your heart, where you decide what to let in and what to keep out. This isn't about being "closed off"—it's about being selective. Not everyone deserves to hear your story, and not everyone has earned the right to lean on you every time they need something.

Consider a time when you felt emotionally exhausted after talking to someone. Did you feel pressured to listen because you didn't want to be "the bad friend" or "the difficult family member"? Or maybe you felt drained because you gave more of yourself than you had to give. Recognizing these moments can help you identify where your emotional boundaries have been crossed.

Learning to Say No

Setting emotional boundaries often means getting comfortable with "no." No, you're not available to listen to that rant right now. No, you're not ready to share your personal struggles with someone who might not understand. Remember, "no" is a complete sentence. You don't owe anyone an explanation for prioritizing your mental health.

Mental Boundaries: Honoring Your Thoughts

Mental boundaries are about protecting your beliefs, thoughts, and opinions. They're the limits we set around our right to think and express ourselves freely. Have you ever felt pressured to change your opinion just to avoid conflict? Or been made to feel small because your beliefs didn't align with someone else's? These experiences often point to a mental boundary being crossed.

Think about the freedom to explore your own ideas and opinions as sacred ground. It's one thing to engage in healthy debate, but it's another to feel bullied into silence or doubt. Mental boundaries help us maintain our autonomy and individuality—they remind us that we don't have to be anyone but ourselves, and we don't have to agree with others to be respected.

Recall a time when someone tried to impose their beliefs on you, or made you feel "less than" for what you think or believe. How did that make you feel? Did you end up questioning yourself?

Recognizing these experiences can help you see where your mental boundaries need reinforcing.

Standing Firm in Your Beliefs
Setting mental boundaries means embracing the fact that you are entitled to your own thoughts. You're not obligated to justify your beliefs or explain your choices to anyone. If someone tries to push their opinions on you, it's okay to say, "I hear you, but this is where I stand."

Reflecting on Boundary Crossings: Recognize Patterns
One of the most powerful exercises in identifying your boundaries is to reflect on situations where you've felt uncomfortable, disrespected, or drained. Start by thinking back to specific interactions—who was involved, what happened, and how it made you feel. Did you feel a pit in your stomach? Did you brush it off, or did it linger with you afterward? These moments are like boundary checkpoints. They show us where we're feeling overextended or undervalued.

To help recognize patterns in boundary crossings, ask yourself:

1. Who consistently ignores my boundaries?
2. What situations leave me feeling exhausted or anxious?
3. Are there people in my life who expect too much from me emotionally, physically, or mentally?

Learning from Boundary Crossings
When you notice these patterns, don't be afraid to make changes. Sometimes, this means setting firmer limits with certain people or situations, even if it feels uncomfortable at first. Every time you reinforce a boundary, you're teaching others how to treat you—and teaching yourself that you're worthy of respect and care.

Embracing Your Right to Boundaries

Setting and honoring boundaries is a bold act of self-love. It can be challenging, especially if you're used to putting everyone else first, but remember that every time you say "no" to something that doesn't serve you, you're saying "yes" to your own worth.

Boundaries aren't about keeping people out; they're about inviting the right people in—the ones who respect your space, your time, and your heart. So take a deep breath, tune into what you need, and start creating the boundaries that honor who you truly are.

"The most important thing is to be yourself. I have always had to learn how to take care of myself, because if I'm not healthy, nothing else can be."

Alicia Keys

3.2 Communicating Boundaries Assertively

Understand Your Communication Style

Before we dive into practical tools, let's take a moment to reflect on your current communication style. Do you tend to avoid conflict, holding back on expressing your true feelings? Or do you sometimes overreact, maybe speaking up too harshly or defensively?

Recognizing your communication style is essential for growth. According to communication theory, understanding and adjusting your style improves the clarity of your message and reduces misinterpretations (Hargie, 2011).

Common Communication Styles and How They Affect Boundaries:

- *Passive:* Often, a passive communicator feels it's "safer" to stay quiet rather than risk disagreement. The downside? Your needs go unmet, and over time, resentment builds. Passive communicators might say things like, "I don't mind," when they absolutely do mind.

- *Aggressive*: On the flip side, aggressive communication involves expressing yourself at the expense of others. It might look like interrupting, talking over someone, or using intimidating body language. While aggressive communicators may get their point across, it often comes at the cost of trust and connection.

- *Passive-Aggressive:* This style is like a mix of passive communication with underlying resentment. You might not directly express your frustration, but it shows up indirectly— like through sarcasm, "forgetting" commitments, or giving the silent treatment.

- *Assertive:* Assertive communication, which we'll focus on developing, is about openly and respectfully expressing your thoughts, feelings, and needs. It's about saying, "I deserve to be heard," without stepping on anyone else's right to do the same. Assertive communication fosters mutual respect and builds a foundation for trust.

A study on relationship dynamics found that assertive communication significantly increases relationship satisfaction because it reduces misunderstandings and promotes honesty (Leary et al., 2007). Moving towards assertive communication is powerful, and it's a skill anyone can develop with practice and patience.

Technique 1: The "I" Statement – Speak About Your Feelings, Not Their Behavior

The "I" statement technique is a powerful way to own your feelings without placing blame or provoking defensiveness in others. It's a cornerstone of assertive communication because it shifts the focus from the other person's behavior to your experience.
Developed as part of nonviolent communication (NVC), this method has been shown to promote empathy and reduce conflict (Rosenberg, 2003).

An "I" statement follows a simple structure:

- *"I feel [emotion] when [situation] because [reason]. I need [need]."*

Breaking down this formula can be incredibly freeing. Imagine feeling upset when a friend cancels plans last minute. Instead of saying, "You're always flaking on me!" (which is likely to provoke defensiveness), you could say:

- *"I feel disappointed when plans change unexpectedly because I was really looking forward to our time together. I need a little more notice so I can plan my time."*

Why This Works:

When you use "I" statements, you take responsibility for your emotions, which can help the other person understand your perspective without feeling attacked. This is especially important in close relationships, where it's easy to unintentionally hurt each other. According to communication studies, "I" statements help prevent escalation and create a space for mutual respect and understanding (Eddy, 2012).

Practice Scenarios

Let's look at a few more scenarios to see how "I" statements can work in different contexts:

- *Personal Space Boundary:* "I feel uncomfortable when people stand very close to me because I value my personal space. I need a little more room to feel comfortable."
- *Emotional Boundary:* "I feel overwhelmed when we talk about such personal topics early on. I need to establish some boundaries around these conversations."

As you practice, you'll notice how "I" statements make conversations smoother and allow for more honest connection. They create room for others to understand where you're coming from, making boundary-setting feel more natural.

Technique 2: The Broken Record – Reaffirming Your Boundary Consistently

Let's talk about persistence. The "broken record" technique is exactly what it sounds like—repeating your boundary calmly and consistently, like a broken record, whenever it's tested. This technique can feel awkward at first, but it's incredibly effective for setting boundaries with people who push back.

Why Repetition Works

There's science behind why this works. Repetition reinforces the boundary in the other person's mind and makes it clear that you're serious. Studies in communication show that repetition helps establish clarity and reinforces resolve (Albrecht & Bachman, 1997).

Using the Broken Record Technique Imagine a coworker who constantly asks you to stay late. You've made it clear that your evenings are for family time, but they keep asking. Here's how you can apply the broken record technique:

- Coworker: "Can you stay late? We're short-staffed."
- You: "I appreciate the need, but I have commitments in the evening."
- Coworker: "Come on, it's just this once."
- You: "I understand, but I have commitments in the evening."

Each time you repeat your boundary, you're reinforcing it without engaging in a long debate. The calm repetition shows that you're serious, making it harder for the other person to argue against your boundary.

Practice Scenarios

- Family Boundary: If family members push you to discuss a topic you're uncomfortable with, repeat: "I'm not comfortable discussing that."
- Work Boundary: If your boss pressures you to work weekends, calmly reiterate: "I need my weekends for personal time."

Each time you hold firm, you're reinforcing your right to have boundaries. And over time, others will learn to respect them because they'll understand you mean what you say.

Technique 3: The Sandwich Method – Wrapping Your Boundary in Positivity

The "sandwich method" is an excellent technique for delivering boundaries with a positive frame. This technique is particularly helpful in situations where you want to maintain harmony or soften the message. The sandwich method has been shown to increase receptivity and make even difficult messages easier to accept (Blader & Tyler, 2003).

Breaking Down the Sandwich Method The method involves three simple steps:

1. Positive Start: Begin with a compliment or positive acknowledgment.
2. Boundary Statement: State your boundary clearly.
3. Positive End: Conclude with encouragement or reassurance.

Example

Let's say a friend keeps asking you to go out late, but you need your evenings to recharge:

- *Start*: "I love that you want to spend time together."
- *Boundary:* "I need to be in bed by 10 to feel my best, so I can't stay out too late."
- *End:* "I'd still love to spend time with you. Let's plan something earlier!"

The sandwich method is gentle but effective because it wraps your boundary in positivity, helping the other person see that your "no" isn't personal. It shows you care while being honest about what you need.

Practice Scenarios

- Friend Boundary: If a friend asks for too much emotional support: "I'm glad you trust me, but I need to take a step back tonight. I know you're strong and can work through this."
- Work Boundary: If a colleague keeps offloading tasks: "I admire your work, but I need to keep my focus on my own tasks. I know you'll handle this well."

Using the sandwich method ensures you're gentle without compromising on your needs.

Technique 4: Using Neutral Language – Stay Calm and Centered

The words you choose matter, and neutral language is a powerful tool in setting boundaries without escalating conflict. Neutral language means choosing words that don't imply blame, judgment, or emotion. It's a way to keep the conversation grounded and constructive.

Why Neutral Language Matters

Studies show that people are more likely to respond calmly and openly to feedback when it's presented without emotional charge or accusatory tones (Leary, 2007). By using neutral language, you maintain control of your emotions and prevent conversations from veering.

In essence, setting boundaries is a powerful way to honor and protect yourself. Techniques like "I" statements, the broken record, and neutral language help you express your needs confidently and respectfully. Boundaries foster healthier relationships and remind you—and others—that your needs truly matter.

"You only get one life. You should do what makes you feel alive, not what you think other people expect you to do."

Mindy Kaling

3.3 Understanding Healthy vs. Unhealthy Dynamics

Let's dive deeper into what makes a relationship healthy. We've all been in relationships where we've felt drained, uncertain, or unappreciated. But recognizing the traits of healthy relationships can give us a roadmap for what to look for—and more importantly, what to walk away from. Healthy relationships don't just happen; they are created through mutual understanding, respect, and effort. When both people are aligned with these principles, the relationship thrives.
So, let's break down the key characteristics that make a relationship healthy, from a place of mutual respect to empathy and beyond.

1. Mutual Respect:

The Foundation of Everything
If a relationship is built on respect, it's solid ground. You're not just there for the good times; you're there to honor each other's space, opinions, and individuality. Respect isn't a one-time thing —it's about how you speak to each other, how you act when the other person is upset, how you deal with misunderstandings. It's about recognizing the humanity in each other, acknowledging each other's differences, and being willing to grow together.

Think about it: in a healthy relationship, you don't feel like you have to shrink yourself. You can show up as your full self, even when you're flawed or imperfect. Your flaws are not met with shame but with understanding. When you disagree, respect still guides the conversation. There's no yelling, no name-calling, no belittling. You just disagree, express your points of view, and move forward with grace.

Example: A healthy partner or friend wouldn't go behind your back and spread rumors about you. Instead, they'd speak to you directly about an issue, in a manner that's respectful to you as a person. They listen to you, not just to wait for their turn to speak but to truly understand where you're coming from.

2. Supportive Growth: Elevating Each Other

Growth in a relationship isn't just about getting better at your communication skills or learning to do more laundry. It's about both parties *helping each other become the best version of themselves.* Healthy relationships encourage growth and empowerment. You don't just put up with each other's dreams; you actively *support and celebrate them.*

Being part of a healthy dynamic means you aren't afraid to step out of your comfort zone, because you know you have someone by your side who's willing to cheer you on. They see your potential—sometimes even before you do—and they're not afraid to help you realize it. There's no resentment when the other person succeeds; rather, it's celebrated together.

Example: When you decide to go back to school or start that side business, a healthy friend or partner won't make you feel guilty for wanting more. They'll say, "Yes! Do it! Let's figure out how we can support this dream."

3. Honest Communication: Cutting Through the BS

We all know that communication is key, but it's also about how you communicate. Healthy relationships aren't about constant sunshine and rainbows. They're about dealing with the storms together. This requires open, honest conversations, even when the truth is uncomfortable.

Honest communication means you can share how you really feel —without fear of retaliation or guilt. It means you're willing to have hard conversations, but in ways that respect the other person's feelings. There's no manipulation, no passive-aggressive remarks. You simply talk through the issues, without fear of retribution or unnecessary drama. When someone can say exactly what they feel without fear of being judged or punished, that's emotional freedom. That's a relationship that works.

Example: If something's bothering you, a healthy relationship allows you to speak up without it turning into a catastrophe. You can say, "I've been feeling neglected lately. Let's talk about it," and the other person will listen, not just defend themselves.

4. Respecting Boundaries: Setting and Holding Them Firm
This is a big one—probably one of the most important elements. Boundaries aren't just about saying "no" when you don't want to do something; it's about protecting your physical, emotional, and mental space. When both parties in a relationship understand each other's limits and needs, they make room for mutual respect.

A healthy relationship means understanding that boundaries are *non-negotiable.* If someone crosses your boundaries, whether they're physical (invading your personal space) or emotional (being dismissive of your feelings), it's time to have a conversation.
A healthy partner or friend doesn't pressure you to go beyond your comfort zone—they work within your limits and ensure the space between you is *safe and sacred.*

Example: If you need time alone to recharge, a healthy friend or partner won't guilt-trip you for taking a break. They'll respect that time and, in turn, encourage you to take care of yourself.

5. Empathy: The Heart of Compassion
In healthy relationships, empathy is everything. Empathy is about truly understanding where the other person is coming

from, not just offering solutions or brushing their feelings aside. Healthy relationships allow for both people to feel heard. If someone is going through a tough time, empathy means you don't tell them how they should feel or fix the problem for them. You just listen and allow them to feel without judgment.

There's something incredibly powerful about being in a relationship where both people understand each other's emotional language. It creates a deep sense of connection and trust. Empathy allows you to be vulnerable, knowing that the other person will hold your feelings with care, not with judgment or disdain.

Example: When you're having a rough day and you spill your heart out, a healthy partner or friend won't try to "fix" you but will say something like, "I hear you. That sounds really tough. How can I support you?"

Identifying Relationships That Limit You vs. Those That Support You

Now that we've covered the hallmarks of healthy relationships, let's take a deeper dive into identifying those relationships that *drain* you, limit your growth, and leave you feeling empty. Relationships that limit you aren't always easy to spot—they can sneak up on you, disguised as friendships, family, or romantic partnerships that seem to care. But the reality is, these are relationships that hold you back from becoming the person you're meant to be. Let's dive deeper into how to spot them.

1. Energy Vampires: The Silent Drainers

Have you ever walked away from a conversation feeling like you just ran a marathon but without the runner's high? Energy vampires suck the life out of you, often without even realizing it. These are the people who demand your attention and energy but never offer the same in return. They're always "needing" something, whether it's validation, sympathy, or a constant shoulder to cry on. And while you can certainly be supportive, you shouldn't be carrying someone else's emotional weight indefinitely.

Example: Your friend calls you every day to complain about their toxic relationship. You listen and offer advice, but all they do is complain—without any change. After a while, you begin to feel emotionally drained, like you're giving and giving but getting nothing back.

2. *Unreciprocated Effort: The One-Sided Relationships*
Have you ever found yourself the only one reaching out, planning activities, or keeping the relationship alive? That's a huge red flag. Relationships—of any kind—are a two-way street. Healthy relationships are about equal investment. You both put in the work, whether it's time, effort, or emotional energy.

Example: You're the one texting first. You're the one planning the hangouts. You're the one putting in the effort to stay connected. After a while, this becomes exhausting and leaves you feeling unappreciated.

3. *Shaming and Belittling: The Silent Killers of Self-Worth*
No one should ever make you feel less than for being who you are. Shaming or belittling comments chip away at your self-esteem. They make you question your worth and your place in the world. If someone consistently makes you feel like you're "too much" or "not enough," it's a sign that the relationship is not healthy.

Example: You've been working hard to lose weight or get healthier, and your so-called friend makes snide comments like, "Wow, you've been working out so much, but I don't see much of a difference." That's not supportive. That's cruel and demoralizing.

4. Gaslighting and Manipulation: The Hidden Abuse
Gaslighting is one of the most insidious forms of abuse because
it makes you question your own reality. If someone constantly
manipulates you into doubting yourself or makes you feel crazy
for trusting your feelings, it's time to get out. Manipulative
behavior often hides behind nice words or fake affection, but the
effect it has on you is devastating.

Example: Your partner tells you that you're overreacting to
something they did, even though you have clear evidence of the
situation. When you try to explain how you feel, they twist the
story until you start wondering if you're just imagining things.

5. Constant Drama and Conflict: The Drama Addicts
Healthy relationships don't thrive on drama. They don't revolve
around constant arguing, passive-aggressive behavior, or
confusion. If your relationship is like a rollercoaster of highs and
lows, where the peace is always followed by an argument or
unresolved tension, then it's draining your energy and emotions.

Example: A friend who constantly starts drama or plays games
to get attention keeps the relationship in a state of chaos. You
find yourself constantly walking on eggshells, never knowing
what to expect.

Healthy relationships are built on respect, empathy, trust, and
mutual growth. They empower you, allow you to be your true
self, and create space for both individuals to thrive. On the other
hand, relationships that limit you drain your energy, stifle your
growth, and leave you feeling unappreciated. Recognizing these
patterns is crucial for creating a life filled with relationships that
nourish and support you. When you set boundaries and love
yourself, you naturally attract those who will honor and value
you, leading to deeper, healthier connections.

"Love yourself first and everything else falls into line."

Rihanna

3.4 Detaching from Toxic Relationships

Let's be real—getting rid of toxic relationships is not like flipping a switch. It's messy, emotional, and feels like walking through molasses while you're trying to run a marathon. Whether it's a toxic friendship, family dynamic, or an emotionally draining romantic relationship, detaching isn't just about cutting someone off on social media (though, let's be honest, that can feel satisfying). It's about doing the work inside of yourself. It's about recognizing the unhealthy emotional bonds, understanding why you stayed stuck in the first place, and finally, learning how to let go.

1. Acknowledging the Emotional Tie
Before you can even think about cutting the cord, you have to first realize that there's a cord in the first place. You might not even know how deep these emotional ties are until you start taking a closer look at your reactions and feelings. Are you constantly feeling drained, anxious, or guilty? Does this person have an unhealthy amount of control over your emotional state? You might be tangled in a toxic dynamic without even realizing the extent of it.
These emotional ties can often be disguised as loyalty, love, or even fear. But here's the thing—real love doesn't leave you constantly questioning your worth, second-guessing your decisions, or feeling like a damn emotional sponge.
So, let's get clear. Recognize the signs of unhealthy emotional attachment:

- *The people-pleasing cycle:* You're constantly adjusting your needs to keep the peace, even when it costs you your happiness or energy.

- *Guilt and shame:* You feel guilty for asserting your needs or boundaries, and you're made to feel like you're the problem.

- *Emotional manipulation:* You feel like you're walking on eggshells, not knowing what mood they'll be in next or what you'll do to "fix" things.

It's okay to admit that you're caught in this cycle. Recognizing it is the first step to freedom.

2. The Emotional Work of Letting Go

You've probably heard the phrase "let it go" a million times. And every time you hear it, you want to scream, "If it were that easy, I'd already be done!" But the thing is, letting go of emotional attachments is not about *forcing* yourself to forget or just saying, "I'm done." It's about acknowledging the grief, anger, sadness, or fear that comes with it.

Feel your feelings.
Allow yourself to feel angry, hurt, disappointed—*whatever* you're feeling. It's not about bypassing those feelings; it's about processing them. You don't have to apologize for your emotions. You're not weak or "dramatic" for feeling hurt. You're human. And once you fully experience these feelings, you can start to untangle the emotional knots.

3. Understanding the Roots of the Emotional Attachment

When you begin the process of letting go, it's crucial to understand *why* you're emotionally tied to this person. Did you grow up in a home where love felt conditional? Are you afraid of being alone or abandoned? Do you feel responsible for their happiness? These root causes often come from past experiences and can be hard to shake, but they *can* be healed. And *you* can do the healing.

Take a moment to ask yourself these questions:
- *Why did I allow myself to stay in this relationship for so long?*

- *What is it about them or their behavior that I keep excusing or rationalizing?*
- *Do I feel responsible for their happiness or wellbeing?*

Understanding the roots of your attachment helps you separate your identity from the relationship. Because at the end of the day, you are not the sum of other people's actions, behaviors, or feelings.

4. The Power of Boundaries in Detaching

When we talk about detaching, we often talk about cutting ties or walking away. But detaching also means learning how to protect your peace while still navigating the relationship. If completely cutting someone off isn't an option (yet), boundaries are your best friend. They allow you to interact without losing yourself.

Boundary-setting techniques that will help you manage the relationship while you're still processing the emotional detachment:

- *The "Grey Rock" Method:* This is a technique where you become emotionally neutral when interacting with someone who drains you. Be as boring as a grey rock. Don't engage in emotional conversations or drama. Be polite but emotionally distant. Over time, this will make them lose interest in trying to manipulate you or pull you into their chaos.

- *Physical Distance:* Sometimes, emotional detachment requires physical space. If you can, create some distance in your interactions. Limit phone calls, reduce face-to-face time, and step back when the relationship is starting to feel suffocating.

- *Acknowledge the Need for Change:* Accept that things can no longer be the same, and let go of the illusion that you can "fix" the relationship. You may have to face the painful truth that it's time to change how you relate to them.

*5. **The Importance of Self-Love in the Detaching Process***
Let me say it loud and clear: You cannot fully detach from a toxic relationship if you don't love yourself. The reason you stayed in that toxic pattern in the first place is because there was a part of you that believed you didn't deserve better. Maybe you thought you didn't deserve peace, respect, or love—hell, you might've even believed that all relationships are chaotic.

But here's the thing: the more you love yourself, the less tolerance you'll have for being treated poorly.

When you start honoring yourself, recognizing your worth, and respecting your boundaries, you create the strength to detach from toxicity. No one can make you feel small if you don't give them that power.

*6. **Taking Action: Cutting Ties & Moving Forward***
The final piece of the puzzle is taking action. Once you've processed your emotions, understood your attachment, and set your boundaries, it's time to cut the ties.
Now, this doesn't mean you have to be cruel or disrespectful about it. You can still honor the relationship for what it was, but you don't have to allow it to continue to take from you.

Practical steps for cutting ties respectfully:

- ***Have the conversation*** (if necessary). Let the person know that you need space or that you're no longer available for the kind of relationship that was happening. Keep it short, direct, and clear. No need to apologize or explain yourself endlessly.

- ***Declutter your emotional space.*** After the conversation (or even if the person isn't receptive), start to distance yourself emotionally. Remove them from your daily thoughts. You don't need to keep track of everything they're doing or thinking.

- ***Focus on your healing.*** Fill your space with things that make you feel good—self-care routines, journaling, spending time with people who lift you up, and activities that inspire you.

Letting go of unhealthy emotional ties is not easy. But it is *necessary*. It's not about rejecting the person; it's about rejecting the way they make you feel about yourself. It's about reclaiming your energy, your peace, and your emotional health. When you release these toxic attachments, you make room for healthier, more fulfilling relationships with people who *see* you, *value* you, and support your growth.
Remember, you are worthy of relationships that make you feel seen, heard, and respected. It's time to stop investing in those who only take from you, and start building the life and the connections you truly deserve.

"Don't ever speak negatively about yourself. Speak kindly and lovingly to yourself. You are the most important person in your life."

Tina Fey

3.4 Fostering Meaningful Connections

Cultivating Relationships That Add Value to Your Life
In this era of superficial connections and endless scrolls through social media feeds, it's easy to feel like you're surrounded by people—but are they truly adding value to your life? Or are they just occupying space? This is the kind of question you need to ask yourself. And when you start asking, you might just discover that not all relationships are as nourishing as they should be.

You don't need to apologize for being picky about the people you let into your life. You have every right to choose those who genuinely uplift you, who challenge you to be your best self, and who make you feel like the world is yours to conquer. So let's dive into how you can intentionally surround yourself with the right people—those who truly inspire and elevate you.

1. *Recognizing What Truly Adds Value*
Think of value in terms of how someone contributes to your life in the long run. Do they challenge your mindset? Do they encourage you to chase your dreams, or do they keep you stuck in a cycle of fear and self-doubt?
When you start reflecting on this, you might find that there are relationships in your life that have become stagnant—like a pool of water that hasn't been stirred in ages. It might have once been refreshing, but now it's grown stale. Value-based relationships, on the other hand, are more like a bubbling spring: ever-flowing, ever-nourishing, and ever-expanding. It's not about quantity—it's about quality. Just like that old saying, "If you want to go fast, go alone; if you want to go far, go together." The people who will walk with you to greater heights will help you thrive.

2. *The Power of Uplifting Connections*
Now, let's get down to the nitty-gritty of how to surround yourself with people who elevate you. This doesn't happen by

accident. You must actively cultivate an environment of growth, inspiration, and shared values. So how do you begin?

- *Assess the Current Landscape:* First, take a hard look at your existing relationships. Which ones leave you feeling energized? Which ones drain you? It's important to be brutally honest here—some relationships are toxic, and others are just... meh. It's okay to outgrow people. No one should be offended if you're growing, as long as you're doing it with respect and integrity. Take note of who brings out the best in you, and who brings out the worst.

- *Quality Over Quantity:* Contrary to the popular belief that you need a huge circle to succeed, the most successful and impactful people often have a small group of trusted individuals. You don't need to have a hundred friends—you need a few solid ones who genuinely believe in you, your potential, and who have your back.

- *Embrace People Who Challenge You (In a Positive Way):* One of the most profound forms of support you can receive is from people who challenge you to think bigger, reach higher, and push through your comfort zones. These are the kinds of people who will question you—not to break you down, but to help you expand. They're the ones who will tell you when you're playing small, or when you're hiding from your potential. That's the kind of energy you want around you.

3. The Role of Shared Values and Goals

You're not going to vibe with everyone, and that's okay. You shouldn't have to. Shared values and goals are a major factor when it comes to cultivating relationships that add value. Think about the people who are in your life now—are you aligned on what truly matters to you?

- Shared Interests: You don't have to be identical to your friends or partners, but it's critical to share some key values. Are you both passionate about self-growth? Do you want to create impact in the world? Do you want to live a fulfilling life or are they still stuck in a mindset of scarcity and settling for mediocrity? If your goals don't align, there's going to be a disconnect sooner or later.

- Support, Not Competition: The right people will never feel threatened by your success. Instead, they'll celebrate it. They will cheer for you because your victories are their victories. If someone feels the need to undermine you or create competition unnecessarily, that's a red flag. Healthy relationships thrive on collaboration, not comparison.

- Mutual Respect: You should never feel like you're "too much" for someone. If your dreams, ideas, or ambitions intimidate others in your life, it might be time to reconsider the relationship. True connections are built on mutual respect—not just for what you've accomplished, but for who you are as a person. It's about accepting each other's quirks, strengths, and flaws without judgment.

4. Cultivating Positive Energies

Okay, now that we've talked about the principles of value-based relationships, let's focus on some tangible ways to attract the right people. It starts with you. If you want to surround yourself with individuals who inspire and elevate, you must also work on becoming the person who inspires and elevates.

Be the Energy You Want to Attract: Look, if you're constantly grumpy, closed off, or insecure, you're not going to draw in people who are positive and uplifting. The law of attraction works both ways. If you want the kind of people who will bring light into your life, you have to be willing to shine. Start embracing your own growth and joy—people who are on the same wavelength will gravitate toward you.

Create Your Own Tribe: This doesn't mean you need to join every group on the internet, or hang out with every single person who crosses your path. Focus on cultivating genuine, deep relationships with a few. Attend workshops, engage in activities that interest you, and be present. You'll find your people when you're living authentically.

Set Healthy Boundaries: The best way to ensure that people add value to your life is by setting boundaries. You need to teach others how to treat you, and that starts with how you treat yourself. People who respect your space, your energy, and your worth are the ones who will elevate you.

5. *Let the Right People In*

Cultivating relationships that add value is not just about being "nice" or "available." It's about being intentional with the people you let into your life, and actively choosing those who nurture your growth, your ambitions, and your well-being. When you focus on quality over quantity, align yourself with people who share your values and inspire you, and continuously work on becoming the best version of yourself, you'll start to see the incredible power of meaningful connections.

And here's the kicker: You deserve relationships that make you feel supported, valued, and heard. You don't need to settle for anything less. So take a moment, look around, and ask yourself: Are these people bringing out the best in me? If the answer is no —then it's time to make a change. Surround yourself with the ones who elevate you, and watch your world expand in ways you never thought possible.

You are worth it.

"Beauty is how you feel inside, and it reflects in your eyes. It is not something physical."

Sophia Loren

4. Crafting a Positive Mindset

4.1 Understanding the Power of Your Thoughts

Alright, let's pause for a moment and take a deep breath. I know, we're talking about something that can be a little overwhelming, but bear with me, because once you truly understand this concept, it can change your life.

Your thoughts—they're not just fluff, background noise, or random fleeting moments in your brain. They are the foundation of everything you experience. Every emotion you feel, every action you take, and the reality you create around you is, in large part, shaped by the thoughts you choose to entertain.

This isn't some fluffy, feel-good, "just think positive and everything will magically be fine" kind of conversation. This is about getting to the root of who you are, what you believe, and how that has been directly influencing your emotional landscape, your self-worth, and ultimately your life.

Let's dive deep and really unpack the power of your thoughts.

The Science Behind Your Thoughts

Before we dive into all the ways that your thoughts affect your emotions and actions, let's take a moment to understand what's actually happening in your brain. You see, when you think a thought, it's not just an abstract concept floating in your head— it's a physical process.

Your brain is firing neurons, making connections, and creating neural pathways based on the thoughts you entertain. These pathways are like grooves in the brain that get deeper and stronger the more you think a particular thought. The more you think something, the easier it is to think it again. Over time, these patterns become automatic, which is why we tend to think the same things day in and day out without realizing it.

And here's where it gets interesting: The brain doesn't distinguish between positive and negative thoughts in terms of how much energy they take. Whether you're thinking, "I am unstoppable" or "I am a failure," the brain is still working, making those neural connections.

But what you're feeding your mind determines the quality of the energy you're creating. If you're constantly thinking about your inadequacies, your mistakes, or the things you wish you could change, you are training your brain to reinforce those negative neural pathways. The more you think those thoughts, the more ingrained they become. And the more ingrained they become, the more they shape your reality.

This is why the work you do on your mindset is so powerful. When you begin to intentionally think positive, empowering, and supportive thoughts, you start rewiring your brain. You begin to create new neural pathways that support your growth, your confidence, and your capacity to achieve your dreams.

How Thoughts Shape Emotions, Actions, and Well-Being

Now that we understand a bit about the science behind it, let's explore how these thoughts impact your life. Because let's face it: We all know that what goes on inside our heads doesn't stay there. It shows up in how we feel, how we act, and ultimately, in the life we create for ourselves.

Thoughts Lead to Emotions

The relationship between your thoughts and emotions is like an unbreakable chain. Your thoughts are the first link, and they are the driving force that determines how you feel. For example, let's say you think, "I'm not good enough to go after that promotion." That thought immediately triggers an emotion— maybe fear, insecurity, or doubt. And from that place, you're not going to feel empowered to act. You might feel small, defeated, and totally drained. Your self-esteem takes a hit, and your entire emotional state starts to spiral.

You become overwhelmed with feelings of inadequacy. Your body may even respond—your heart rate rises, your stomach tightens, and you may feel that pit of anxiety. But it all started with that thought.

It's not just about career-related thoughts. Think about how often you've had a negative thought about your body, your relationships, or your future. Maybe you think, "I'll never find someone who loves me," or "I'm just not attractive enough." Again, those thoughts send a ripple effect through your emotional state. Negative thoughts are like magnets—they attract more negativity. When you entertain them, they affect how you feel.

But this is where the power comes in. Just like negative thoughts lead to negative emotions, positive thoughts lead to positive emotions. If you think, "I am worthy of love and happiness," your emotional state shifts. You start to feel more confident, more optimistic, and more empowered. And with that elevated emotional state, you're more likely to take inspired actions that align with your goals.

Thoughts Influence Actions

Let's say you're telling yourself, "I'm a failure, I never get anything right." Do you think that kind of thought will get you out of bed and take bold action toward your dreams? Hell no. That thought will paralyze you. It will make you question your every move, and it will stop you from trying. When you believe you're incapable or unworthy, your actions will mirror that belief. You won't take the necessary steps to get where you want to go because, deep down, you've already convinced yourself it's impossible.

On the flip side, when you start thinking, "I'm capable of handling whatever comes my way," or "I may not know everything yet, but I'm learning," your actions change. You begin to take bold steps. You start making moves, even when you don't have it all figured out. You show up for yourself, and that's when the magic happens.

Your thoughts set the stage for the actions you'll take. If your thoughts are negative, your actions will likely be self-sabotaging. If your thoughts are positive, you'll take empowered steps toward your goals. This isn't some mystical, "just think it and it will happen" kind of approach. This is about creating a mindset that allows you to show up for yourself in the most powerful, resilient way possible.

Thoughts Shape Your Overall Well-Being
Your thoughts shape not only your actions and emotions but also your physical and mental well-being. When you're stuck in a loop of negative thoughts, stress hormones like cortisol flood your body. This leads to increased anxiety, poor sleep, a lack of motivation, and can even affect your immune system. Prolonged negative thinking can result in burnout, exhaustion, and a constant state of dissatisfaction with life. Your thoughts literally make you sick, both emotionally and physically.

On the other hand, when you focus on positive, empowering thoughts, your body responds differently. You feel more energized. Your stress levels decrease. You sleep better. You start to experience greater mental clarity, more optimism, and a general sense of calm. You can't separate your mental state from your physical health. Your body listens to everything your mind says.

Identifying and Changing Negative Thought Patterns
Now that we know how thoughts impact everything, it's time to talk about how you can stop those negative thoughts from running your life. Because let's be honest—if you don't actively change your thought patterns, they will continue to control you.

Here's the thing about negative thought patterns: They're
sneaky. They can show up when you least expect them, and
before you know it, you've spiraled into a negative headspace
that feels impossible to escape from. But guess what? You have
the power to take back control. Let's talk about how.

- ***Step 1:** Become the Observer of Your Thoughts*

The first step to changing your thoughts is becoming aware of
them. Most people walk around on autopilot, unaware of how
much negative self-talk is happening in the background. You
might not even realize how often you're criticizing yourself or
doubting your worth.

So the first step in the process is to become the observer of your
own mind. Start noticing when negative thoughts arise. Keep a
journal by your bedside and write down the thoughts that come
up throughout the day. You'll start to notice patterns.

Are there recurring themes? Do you tend to criticize your
appearance or your abilities? Do you always doubt yourself
when it comes to taking risks? Write these thoughts down.
Awareness is the first step in changing anything.

- ***Step 2:** Challenge the Negative Thoughts*

Once you've identified a negative thought, challenge it. I want
you to look at that thought, dissect it, and ask yourself, "Is this
really true?" Most of the time, you'll realize that the negative
thought you've been thinking isn't based on any real evidence.
It's simply an old belief that's been ingrained in your mind over
time.

For example, you might think, "I'm not good enough to get the
job I want." But when you take a step back, you realize that you
have the skills, experience, and potential to excel. Maybe you've
just never given yourself enough credit. Challenge those
thoughts. You deserve to believe in your own abilities.

- *Step 3: Reframe Your Thoughts*

Now that you've identified and challenged the negative thought, it's time to reframe it. This doesn't mean just plastering a fake smile and pretending everything is fine when it's not. Reframing means taking a negative thought and flipping it into something more empowering. If your mind is telling you, "I'm not good enough," replace it with, "I am enough, just as I am." If you think, "I'll never succeed," reframe it to, "I am capable of success, and I'm taking steps every day to get closer to my goals."

It's about consciously choosing a more empowering thought, one that supports your growth and aligns with your desires. The more you practice this, the easier it becomes to reframe negative thoughts on the fly.

Techniques for Changing Negative Thought Patterns

Now that you've got the foundational understanding, let's talk about specific techniques to help you change your thought patterns. These are practical strategies that will help you rewrite the story you've been telling yourself.

- *1. Affirmations*

Positive affirmations are a powerful tool for shifting your mindset. They are short, positive statements that you can repeat to yourself throughout the day. Affirmations help to reprogram your subconscious mind and reinforce empowering thoughts.

For example:
- "I am worthy of love and success."
- "I am capable of achieving my dreams."
- "I trust myself to make the best decisions."

Say these affirmations out loud in front of a mirror or silently in your head. When you repeat them enough, they become your new truth.

- *2. Visualization*

Visualization is another technique that can help you shift your mindset. It's about vividly imagining yourself living the life you desire, accomplishing your goals, and embodying your highest potential. Close your eyes and picture yourself being confident, successful, and unstoppable. The more you visualize yourself living the life you want, the more your thoughts will begin to align with that vision.

- *3. Practice Gratitude*

Gratitude is a game-changer when it comes to shifting your mindset. When you focus on what's working in your life instead of what's wrong, your brain starts to look for more reasons to be thankful. It trains your mind to focus on the positive, and that positivity starts to expand into all areas of your life.
Keep a gratitude journal and write down three things you're grateful for every day. This simple practice can shift your focus and improve your outlook on life.

Empower Your Mind, Empower Your Life

Your thoughts are powerful, and they shape the life you live. When you learn to master your thoughts and align them with your goals and desires, everything changes. No more letting negative self-talk and limiting beliefs control you. You have the power to change your inner dialogue, to shift from self-doubt to self-love, from fear to confidence, from victimhood to empowerment.

It's time to take control of your thoughts, because when you do, you take control of your life.

"Confidence comes from within and it comes from being proud of who you are and the decisions you make."

Jessica Ennis-Hill

4.2 Developing a Solution-Oriented Mindset

Life has this funny way of throwing things at you when you least expect it. One minute, you're cruising along, feeling on top of the world, and the next, boom—a curveball comes flying your way. A flat tire. A break-up. A missed opportunity. Or worse yet, you can't figure out how you ended up in this situation at all. And here's the thing—when these curveballs happen, we can either choose to stay stuck, or we can pick ourselves up, dust ourselves off, and start looking for the next step. This is the power of shifting your mindset.

But let's be clear: shifting your mindset isn't about putting on a fake smile and pretending everything's fine. It's not about ignoring the messiness of life. It's not about pushing through your emotions without feeling them. It's about deciding that no matter what, you can and will figure things out. You will shift your focus from the problem to the solution, from the chaos to the clarity. This chapter is about giving you the tools to do exactly that.

So let's talk about something that will change the course of your life if you let it: Developing a solution-oriented mindset.

Shifting from a Focus on Problems to Actively Seeking Solutions

Let's have a little heart-to-heart about problems. We all know them. They come in all shapes and sizes. Sometimes they show up as small annoyances, like losing your keys or dealing with a rude person. Other times, they show up as big, life-altering events—health problems, financial struggles, relationship issues. They're the kind of things that feel like they could break you, if you let them.

Here's the truth, life will always have problems. You will never get to a point where you're just cruising along, problem-free.

But here's the secret most people don't realize—problems are not the end. They're not signs that you're failing or that you're unlucky. Problems are opportunities to grow. And the faster you realize that, the faster you can shift your focus from the problem itself to finding a solution.

When you're focused on the problem, all you see is the mess. You get caught in the whirlwind of frustration, confusion, and stress. The problem becomes the center of your universe. It feels overwhelming, like you're drowning in it, and before you know it, you've spent hours—sometimes days—ruminating on everything that's wrong. You might even start to believe the problem is insurmountable, that it's something you're just going to have to live with.

But the moment you make a conscious decision to shift your focus, everything changes. Instead of asking yourself, "Why is this happening to me?" ask, "What can I do about this?" You're no longer a victim of your circumstances. You're a problem-solver. You're a creator, a person who is fully capable of navigating whatever comes your way. That's when the magic happens. That's when you stop feeling helpless and start feeling empowered.

This isn't always going to be easy. But it will be worth it. When you stop dwelling on the problem, you free up your mental and emotional energy to focus on the solution. This means your problem no longer owns you. You're in control.

Steps to Enhance Problem-Solving Skills and Feel Empowered in Difficult Situations

So now that we've established how important it is to shift your focus, let's talk about how you can develop the skills to actually solve problems and feel empowered in the process. This isn't about just "thinking positively" or "hoping for the best." This is about actionable steps you can take to enhance your problem-solving skills and step into your power.

- *1. Acknowledge the Problem—But Don't Marinate in It*
When problems arise, it's easy to fall into a spiral of negativity. Your mind races to worst-case scenarios. You think about everything that could go wrong. But here's the thing—acknowledging the problem is step one. It's about being real with yourself. Denial doesn't help anyone. Trying to pretend that things are fine when they aren't only prolongs the pain.

The key here is to acknowledge the problem, but not to let it consume you. Don't let it define you. When you face a problem head-on, you strip it of its power.
You turn it from this big, scary thing into something you can handle. You don't need to make the problem your entire focus. You just need to recognize that it's there—and then move on to the next step.

- *2. Break Down the Problem into Smaller, Manageable Pieces*
A big problem can feel overwhelming. That's normal. But here's a powerful trick: break it down. The thing about problems is they can feel like this giant, monstrous thing that you'll never be able to tackle. But when you break it into smaller pieces, each individual piece feels much more manageable.

Let's say you're dealing with a financial issue, like overwhelming debt. When you look at it as one massive problem, it can feel like it's never going to end. But when you break it down into smaller, actionable steps—like reviewing your expenses, creating a budget, looking for ways to increase your income—it suddenly feels more doable. You're no longer stuck thinking about the enormity of it all. Instead, you're taking one step at a time, working your way through the challenge.

This is the beauty of breaking problems down: you take away the power they have over you. They go from being these massive, insurmountable obstacles to smaller, manageable tasks. And as you tick off each piece, you'll feel more in control.

- ***3. Shift Your Focus to What You Can Control***

One of the most empowering things you can do is recognize what is within your control and what isn't. Life is filled with things we can't control—other people's actions, the weather, global events, the past. But what you can control is how you respond. You can control your attitude, your behavior, and the steps you take to improve your situation.

For example, if you're stuck in a toxic work environment, you might not be able to control the behavior of your coworkers or your boss. But what you can control is how you manage your stress, how you set boundaries, and how you protect your energy. Maybe that means setting clear work-life boundaries, practicing self-care outside of work, or actively seeking out a healthier job. The key is to stop giving away your power to things you can't control, and instead, focus on what you can do.

When you start to focus on the things you can control, you reclaim your power. You start to see that you have options. You may not be able to control everything, but you are always in control of how you respond.

- ***4. Brainstorm Solutions—And Try Them***

Now comes the fun part. You've acknowledged the problem, broken it down, and focused on what you can control. Next, it's time to get creative. Brainstorm as many possible solutions as you can. Don't limit yourself in this phase. Even the most outlandish ideas are worth considering. This is your time to think outside the box and get innovative.

Once you have a list of solutions, pick one to start with. Don't wait for the perfect solution to magically appear. Pick the one that feels right, and start moving forward. There's no such thing as a perfect solution, and sometimes the only way to figure out what works is by trying. If the first solution doesn't work, that's okay—just adjust, learn from it, and try again.

- *5. Take Action—Even If It's a Small Step*

Action is where most people get stuck. You can have the best solutions in the world, but if you don't take action, nothing changes. Taking action is what creates momentum. It's what keeps you moving forward, even when the road gets bumpy. Start with one small step. You don't have to have everything figured out. Just take the first step. You'll be amazed at how quickly momentum builds once you start moving. And even if that first step doesn't lead to the exact outcome you wanted, you've still learned something. You've moved forward. And that, my friend, is what matters.

- *6. Evaluate and Adjust*

As you take action, you'll encounter new information. You'll learn what works and what doesn't. And guess what? That's okay. The key is to stay flexible. Be open to adjusting your plan as needed. If something doesn't work, pivot. Learn from your mistakes and use that knowledge to make better decisions going forward.

Viewing Challenges as Chances to Learn and Grow

You know what's wild? Life is constantly throwing challenges your way—not because it's trying to break you, but because it's trying to make you stronger. Challenges are opportunities in disguise. They are your chance to learn, to grow, to become more resilient. Every challenge you face is shaping you into the person you're meant to be. And when you embrace that, the whole game changes.

Instead of fearing challenges, start viewing them as the catalysts for growth. Think about the challenges you've already overcome. How did you grow from them? What lessons did you learn? Every challenge has a hidden gift. You just have to be willing to look for it.

When you shift your mindset to see challenges as opportunities, you stop running away from them. You start seeking them out. You start embracing the discomfort, knowing that it's part of the process. And the more you embrace challenges, the more you grow.

Shift from a "Failure" Mindset to a "Learning" Mindset

Failure is not the end of the road. It's part of the process. The sooner you embrace failure as a stepping stone to success, the sooner you'll get out of your own way.

Failure isn't something to be feared. It's something to be celebrated. When you fail, you learn. You discover what doesn't work, and that's invaluable information.

So stop seeing failure as a reflection of your worth, and start seeing it as the feedback it is. It's a lesson. It's a guide to help you get closer to your goal.

Shifting from a failure mindset to a learning mindset is liberating. It frees you from the fear of messing up, and instead, it encourages you to take risks. It tells you that you don't have to be perfect to succeed—you just have to keep trying.

A solution-oriented mindset is the foundation of a life well-lived. It allows you to navigate the inevitable challenges that come your way with confidence and grace. When you shift your focus from the problem to the solution, you empower yourself to take action, learn from your mistakes, and grow stronger every day.

So the next time life throws you a curveball, remember this: you've got the power to turn any problem into an opportunity for growth. You are a creator, a solution-finder, a badass

woman who can handle anything that comes her way.
And as you do, remember that failure isn't an end—it's part of
the process. Every setback is just a lesson in disguise. The key is
to keep moving forward, keep learning, and keep growing.
Because that's how you build the life you deserve.
And trust me, you deserve it.

"It is our choices that show what we
truly are, far more than our abilities."
J.K. Rowling

4.3 Fostering Optimism with Realistic Positivity

Positivity is one of those terms that's thrown around so much that we often forget what it really means. For most, it's been reduced to a simple slogan of "think positive" or "look on the bright side," but these phrases, when taken too literally, can sometimes be toxic. In reality, fostering optimism with a grounded, realistic approach is about understanding that while life can be tough, the way we respond to it shapes everything—our thoughts, our actions, and the course of our lives.

This chapter is all about harnessing the power of optimism—not the shallow, forced positivity that denies the truth of life's struggles, but the kind of optimism that recognizes challenges and still chooses to rise above them. It's about facing your fears, doubts, and setbacks with the inner knowledge that you have the ability to navigate and even thrive in the face of adversity.

The Difference Between Toxic Positivity and a Genuine Positive Outlook

It's essential to clearly distinguish between what's often referred to as "toxic positivity" and a healthy, grounded optimism.

Toxic Positivity:

Toxic positivity is like a bandaid over a wound that needs stitches. It's the kind of mindset that ignores the reality of pain, disappointment, and hardship and insists that you should be "happy" or "grateful" all the time, no matter the situation. It's an attitude that trivializes your struggles and pressures you to "just get over it" or "think happy thoughts."

You've probably encountered it in conversations like these:

- "Don't worry, everything happens for a reason!" (when you're clearly upset)

- "It could be worse, at least you're not insert worse situation here."
- "Just think positive and good things will happen!"

While these statements are well-intentioned, they invalidate your emotions. They attempt to force you into a state of "positivity" that disregards your present emotional experience and your need for a moment of processing and healing. It's as if you're told that your struggles don't matter and that happiness is a choice you should make at all costs, even if it means pushing your true feelings down.

When people practice toxic positivity, they might ignore pain, bury their emotions, and put on a happy face even when things are falling apart. The result? Long-term emotional stress, disconnection from reality, and a sense of loneliness. This type of positivity makes you feel like you can't be "real" or honest about your struggles, which only leads to more pain.

Genuine Positivity:
Genuine positivity, on the other hand, doesn't require you to ignore your struggles or suppress your emotions. It acknowledges that life is difficult, but it helps you see those challenges as opportunities for growth, learning, and resilience.

This kind of positivity is grounded in reality—it's about accepting that life is messy and hard sometimes, but choosing to believe that things will improve. It's about facing the truth, no matter how ugly, and still finding hope.
A genuine positive outlook doesn't force you to reject negative emotions—it invites you to process them and then choose to move forward with optimism. It's about recognizing the balance between acknowledging your pain and finding the strength to rise above it. It encourages self-compassion, emotional honesty, and taking proactive steps to turn things around.

Imagine you're facing a career setback. Maybe you've been overlooked for a promotion or you've been laid off. A toxic positive approach would say, "Oh well, everything happens for a reason!" or "You should be thankful for what you have!" Meanwhile, a genuine positive mindset would acknowledge your disappointment and frustration but also ask, "What can I learn from this experience? What can I do to grow from this and position myself for something better?"

Realistic positivity isn't about sweeping your emotions under the rug—it's about giving them space to breathe, while simultaneously empowering yourself to take control of the situation and grow from it.

Detach from the Need for Immediate Results

In a world where instant gratification is glorified, it's easy to get discouraged when results don't come quickly. The reality, however, is that meaningful change and growth take time. When you expect results to happen immediately, you're setting yourself up for disappointment.

This is where the concept of realistic positivity comes into play —understanding that progress is often slow and incremental. Rather than focusing on the end result, focus on the daily actions that lead to that result. Every little step you take is a win, and over time, those small steps compound into significant changes. Real optimism understands that it's okay to not see immediate results—what matters is the consistent effort, no matter how small.

Now identify an area in your life where you've been impatient for results (whether it's fitness, career, or personal growth). Instead of focusing on when the results will show up, set a habit that you can commit to daily. This could be something as simple as reading for 15 minutes a day or going for a walk. Over time, these actions will yield powerful results.

Change the Narrative: From Victim to Creator
A large part of developing a positive and realistic mindset is shifting from a victim mentality to one of empowerment. It's easy to feel like life is happening to you, especially when faced with challenges or circumstances that feel out of your control. However, one of the most empowering shifts you can make is to stop seeing yourself as a victim of circumstances and start viewing yourself as the creator of your reality.

When you shift from being a victim to a creator, you take responsibility for how you respond to challenges. You recognize that while you can't control everything that happens in life, you have complete control over your reactions and the choices you make moving forward.

"Self-love is the key to all things. It opens doors, builds resilience, and fuels success."

Serena Williams

Short Inspiring Stories of Real Women Who Chose the Self-Love Path

J.K. Rowling (the creator of Harry Potter)

J.K. Rowling's story is the epitome of resilience, grit, and the relentless pursuit of self-worth. Before she became a household name, she was simply Jo—living in a small, drafty flat, recently divorced, raising her young daughter on welfare, and grappling with depression. And yet, even in the darkest moments, she held on to a dream so fragile, so daring, that it became her lifeline. Jo had no cheering squad, no safety net, and not a clue if her story would ever see the light of day. But she did have an old typewriter, a head full of ideas, and a fierce determination to write. What's remarkable isn't just that she wrote a book; it's that she kept writing, pouring out her heart, bit by bit, through all the setbacks, all the rejections. Writing wasn't just an escape —it was her declaration to herself that she mattered, that her voice mattered, even if the rest of the world didn't see it yet. Every step of Jo's journey was paved with obstacles. She received one rejection letter after another, each one an invitation to give up, to believe the critics who told her she wasn't good enough. But Jo didn't fold. She was fighting for something bigger than a bestseller—she was fighting for her own belief in herself. It was that self-love, that unapologetic conviction, that kept her going.

Jo showed us that self-love isn't about loving only the parts of ourselves that are easy or polished. It's about standing by ourselves through the mess, the doubt, and the heartbreak. It's about looking rejection in the eye and saying, "I am not finished yet."

When Bloomsbury finally said "yes" to publishing Harry Potter and the Philosopher's Stone, it wasn't just a triumph in Jo's career; it was a triumph of her spirit. That first book deal didn't transform her life overnight—she wasn't an instant millionaire, and she still had to fight her way up from the very bottom. But it was a start, and she took it, proving that dreams can come true, not because of luck or timing, but because of the relentless love and belief she had for herself and her story.

Her books went on to change the world, but they did more than that—they became a testament to what's possible when a woman decides to trust herself, to believe in herself when no one else does. Jo's journey is a reminder that self-love is what gives you the strength to keep going when things are impossible, painful, and lonely.

J.K. Rowling didn't just create characters who were brave and resilient. She lived it. Her own story was woven into every line of courage, every lesson of love, loyalty, and hope she poured into her books. Her life became the proof that self-love isn't just some feel-good idea. It's an anchor, a necessity, the source of strength to not only survive but to thrive.

And while the world sees her now as a literary legend, Jo's legacy goes beyond her books. She's a woman who showed us that self-love isn't always pretty or easy, but it is powerful beyond measure. She taught us that every dream worth chasing starts with the courage to believe in yourself, to fight for yourself, and to keep going—no matter who or what stands in your way. And there's no greater magic than that.

Brené Brown

Brené Brown's journey is a masterclass in vulnerability, courage, and the unapologetic power of self-love. Today, she's a name practically synonymous with words like "bravery" and "authenticity," but this woman didn't arrive at that place of power through smooth sailing. Nope, Brené Brown's path to self-love started in a raw, imperfect mess—exactly the way it does for all of us.

Brené began her career in the field of social work, digging into the murky, deeply human issues that most of us try to avoid: shame, fear, imperfection. But here's the kicker—she was trying to understand it all intellectually without facing her own vulnerability. Brené had her life together on the outside, but inside, she was terrified. She describes herself as the "queen of control," someone who, for the longest time, believed that being vulnerable was like inviting disaster to a perfectly good party. Sound familiar?

Her big "aha!" moment wasn't the glamorous, world-shifting epiphany you might imagine. It was more like a breakdown—or, as she's called it, a "spiritual awakening." Brené's research on shame and vulnerability started to hit a little too close to home, and for the first time, she had to look in the mirror and face her own armor. She realized that her whole life was built around dodging vulnerability, sidestepping the very things she was researching. It was messy, it was terrifying, and yes, it broke her wide open.

But here's the beauty of it: when Brené leaned into her vulnerability, she found power. She let go of the need to be perfect and started embracing her wonderfully imperfect self. She started to see that self-love wasn't about being strong in the traditional sense—it was about being brave enough to admit you're scared, and then doing the hard things anyway. Self-love wasn't a gentle whisper in the dark; it was a battle cry that said, "I'm worth it, even with all my messy parts."

And let's talk about her TED Talk, shall we? She went up there, put her research on vulnerability out for the world to see, and did it without the armor. Her heart was in her throat, her self-doubt was screaming, but she did it. And the world responded. That talk went viral, not because she was polished or perfect, but because she was real. She laid herself bare on that stage, and in doing so, she invited all of us to drop our masks, to be brave enough to show up as we are.

Brené didn't become the woman she is today by avoiding hard truths. She became who she was meant to be by embracing her own humanity. And in doing so, she's taught us that the only way to real connection and real love, especially with ourselves, is through courageously owning all of it—the scars, the fears, the parts we think make us unworthy.

Her work has gone on to change lives, not because she has all the answers, but because she's a fellow traveler in the messiness of life. She's walked the walk, she's faced the hard stuff, and she's come out the other side. Brené Brown taught us that self-love doesn't mean you stop feeling afraid; it means you feel it and keep going.

So here's to Brené—a woman who proves that self-love isn't always pretty, but it's the only way to real freedom. And if she can do it, so can you.

Ellen DeGeneres

Ellen's story starts in a small town in Louisiana, where she wasn't exactly the "traditional" picture of a young woman—she was funny, quirky, and, let's be real, a little out there. She didn't fit into the neat, little boxes society had created for women, and for a long time, that wasn't something she was proud of. It was something that made her feel like an outsider. But let me tell you—being an outsider? Turns out, it's not a curse; it's a superpower.

When Ellen first started pursuing comedy, it was rough. This was a time when women in comedy weren't exactly getting the recognition they deserved. It was a boys' club, and she wasn't invited. But guess what? She wasn't waiting for an invitation. She made her own damn seat at the table. She hustled, she worked her ass off, and, of course, she used her unique humor to cut through the noise. At first, though, it wasn't glamorous. She was doing stand-up in small clubs, bombing some nights, being told "no" more times than she could count. But you know what she didn't do? She didn't quit. She wasn't going to let a few rejection letters—or a hundred—stop her from doing what she loved.

One of the biggest turning points came when Ellen came out as gay. In 1997, on her own sitcom, Ellen, she made TV history by revealing her true self. Talk about courage. At that time, coming out in the public eye wasn't something most people would dare to do. But Ellen, in her usual fashion, didn't give a flying fuck what anyone thought. She did it because she was done living a life that wasn't true to her. And guess what? The backlash was brutal. People told her career was over. They said no one would ever watch her show again. She was fired, her sitcom was canceled, and she took a huge hit professionally. But Ellen, being Ellen, laughed through the pain. She didn't let the world's opinion of her break her. She just kept going.

That moment? That was her defining moment of self-love. She chose herself. And here's the thing: when you choose yourself, when you love yourself enough to show up as you are—authentic, unfiltered, and maybe a little wild—that's when magic happens. Ellen didn't just bounce back; she thrived. She found a new platform, The Ellen DeGeneres Show, and took the world by storm. She wasn't the same woman anymore. She was stronger. She was her true self, and that made all the difference.

Ellen's career took off after that, but it wasn't just her fame or fortune that changed—she changed. She went from being the woman who feared the judgment of others to becoming the woman who didn't just accept herself but loved herself fiercely. She stopped apologizing for who she was and, in turn, the world started to fall in love with her.

Her story is a reminder that self-love isn't always pretty. It's not about having perfect hair, a flawless body, or never making mistakes. Self-love is about standing in your truth, no matter how messy, uncomfortable, or scary it might be. It's about owning your quirks, your flaws, and saying, "This is me, take it or leave it." Ellen made her own rules, and in doing so, she gave millions of women permission to do the same.

But the truth is, Ellen's path hasn't been all sunshine and rainbows, either. She's been through the wringer—personally and professionally. She's faced criticism, pressure to conform, and the relentless need to constantly be "on." And yet, she's always found her way back to herself. When she was at the peak of her career, after every success, she found herself asking, "Is this enough? Am I enough?" And you know what she realized? That her worth was never tied to her career or her public persona. Her worth came from within. She wasn't looking for validation from others anymore; she was validating herself.

That's what self-love is about—it's not about getting all the external things to prove that you're worthy. It's about realizing you are worthy, right now, exactly as you are. No more, no less. Ellen's story is proof that no matter where you start or how many times you fail, you can always rebuild, always rise stronger, and always, always come back to yourself.

And that's exactly what she did. She has spent her entire career using her platform to spread positivity, acceptance, and love to the world. Her message is simple: be kind to one another, and most importantly, be kind to yourself. It's okay to make mistakes. It's okay to not be perfect. It's okay to fail. Because through it all, you are still enough.

Ellen didn't just become a household name; she became a symbol of what happens when a woman fully embraces herself—flaws, jokes, struggles, and all. She didn't let the world define her. She defined herself.

So, if you're sitting there wondering if you're enough, take a page from Ellen's book. Yes, you are. And if you don't feel it today? That's okay. Keep showing up, keep loving yourself through the hard days, and keep owning your truth. The world will adjust. It always does.

Ellen DeGeneres didn't just make a career out of being funny—she made a career out of being unapologetically herself. And that's a lesson every woman can learn from. So go ahead, embrace your quirks, show up for yourself, and dance through the storms. Your story isn't finished yet.

And who knows? Maybe you'll be the one breaking the next door down.

Jane Goodall

Her story begins in a small town in England where, from a very young age, she was a curious little girl with big dreams. It wasn't about fame or fortune for her. It was about finding her purpose —and in doing so, changing the world forever.

Let's start with the basics: Jane Goodall didn't fit in. She wasn't the "normal" little girl who played with dolls and had tea parties. Instead, she was a wild-eyed, animal-loving nerd, obsessed with one thing: animals. While the other kids were busy pretending to be princesses, Jane was climbing trees, staring into the eyes of birds, and dreaming of a future with chimpanzees. But this wasn't exactly the dream her family had in mind. They were well-meaning but skeptical—her mother even said she'd never get anywhere if she kept thinking about animals all the time.

Sound familiar? You've probably heard people tell you that your dreams are "too big" or "not realistic." They'll say you need to "be practical," "settle down," or "stop being so emotional." Well, Jane Goodall had the same damn messages ringing in her ears. But here's where the magic happens—she didn't listen. She didn't give a flying f*** what the world thought was "practical" for her. She had a fire in her belly, a fire that could never be put out. And so, she decided to go for it. She trusted her gut, believed in her wild, weird, beautiful passion for animals, and let the chips fall where they may.

Now, her first major leap came when she managed to travel to Africa—no fancy credentials, no university degree in hand, just a fierce will and a head full of ambition. Her journey to self-love began the moment she stepped foot on that continent. She didn't just fall in love with the land or the animals; she fell in love with her own ability to make bold choices, even when everyone around her doubted her. She didn't need anyone's permission, she didn't need their approval, and she certainly didn't need their expectations. She had herself, and that was enough.

But let's be real—no one's journey is a smooth ride. And it wasn't all "look at me, I'm making history" moments for Jane. When she first began studying chimpanzees in Tanzania, people —especially men—questioned everything about her: her ability to be taken seriously, her ability to lead a scientific study, her ability to even be out in the field on her own. This was the 1960s, after all, and the scientific community didn't exactly have a lot of faith in women, let alone women doing something unconventional like living with wild animals.

But Jane, being Jane, didn't give a damn. She just kept doing her thing. She sat in the dirt, climbed the trees, and spent years observing chimpanzees, building a connection with them that no one else had ever achieved. She trusted herself to understand these creatures, and in doing so, she became one of the most respected figures in the scientific world. Her work didn't just change the way we understand chimpanzees—it changed the way we understand ourselves. But more than that, it helped her discover something essential about self-love: you are the expert of your own journey, and no one else can define it for you.

Of course, Jane didn't just wake up one day feeling like a badass. She had moments of doubt, fear, and insecurity. She had moments where she questioned whether she was good enough, whether she had what it took. She's human, after all. But those moments? Those moments were part of her journey. Jane realized that self-love isn't about constantly feeling confident or flawless—it's about showing up for yourself, no matter what, and trusting that you have everything inside you to succeed, even on the hard days.

As Jane's research gained international acclaim, her self-love evolved. It wasn't just about trusting her instincts in the field; it was about finding her voice as a woman, as a scientist, and as a global leader for conservation. She wasn't just sitting back, studying chimpanzees; she was speaking out about environmental issues, advocating for animal rights, and changing the way people thought about the planet. Jane became a powerful force for good, using her voice and her platform to make a difference. She was unapologetic about her passion, her message, and her mission—and that is what real self-love looks like.

Through it all, Jane has never stopped doing the work of her heart. She's been honored, celebrated, and recognized across the globe, but she still does the same work she started decades ago: she listens, she learns, and she speaks up. And that's what makes her so damn inspiring. She trusted herself from the beginning. She didn't wait for validation from anyone. She didn't wait until everything was perfect. She just started. She knew she was enough, even when the world didn't see it yet.

So, what's the lesson here? Well, take notes, honey, because this is important. Jane Goodall's journey to self-love wasn't about being perfect or having everything figured out. It wasn't about waiting for the world to tell her she was worthy. It was about her choosing herself—her dreams, her passions, her truth—and going for it, no matter how messy or challenging it got. She trusted that her path was hers alone, and she didn't let anyone or anything steal her joy, her drive, or her purpose.

You're not here to play small. You're here to live big, to live authentically, to step into your power with everything you've got. Jane Goodall's life is a testament to what happens when a woman trusts herself and stays committed to her mission. She didn't just change the world; she changed herself—and in doing so, she showed us that we, too, have the power to change the world.

Maya Angelou

Maya Angelou's early life was filled with trauma. At the age of seven, she was sexually abused by her mother's boyfriend, a tragedy that left her feeling voiceless, broken, and worthless. After the man was arrested, Maya was sent to live with her grandmother in Arkansas, but the scars of her past stayed with her. She went mute for nearly five years. The silence was a reflection of her internal belief that her voice—her very self— didn't matter. But, in the quiet, something began to shift. Maya began to rediscover her worth, piece by piece. And that's when the journey of self-love began.

You see, self-love doesn't come easily when the world tells you that you're not enough. Maya's silence was not just a result of her trauma—it was her mind's way of processing that pain, of retreating into herself because the world outside had been so harsh. But self-love, in its purest form, is about re-learning your value, even when everything around you suggests otherwise. Maya didn't stay silent forever. She found her voice again, and when she did, she didn't just speak—she shouted, she sang, she wrote. Her journey to self-love was marked by a relentless drive to reclaim her voice, her power, and ultimately, her life. Maya Angelou didn't just survive; she thrived, and she did it by learning how to trust herself.

Trusting herself meant making decisions that were right for her, even when others didn't agree. It meant taking chances when fear tried to keep her small. It meant knowing that her story, no matter how painful, had value. Maya became a writer, an activist, a director, and a teacher—all while staying true to her principles, her beliefs, and her worth. She didn't let her past define her; instead, she let her healing shape her future. Self-love isn't just about feeling good; it's about trusting that you have the strength to overcome, the courage to rise again, and the belief that you can achieve your dreams, no matter where you've come from. Maya Angelou trusted in herself to rebuild, to reinvent, and to become the woman we all admire today.

Maya Angelou wasn't just a woman who wrote beautiful words; she was a woman who took up space in a world that often told her she didn't belong. She demanded respect, not because she expected it, but because she knew she deserved it. She didn't apologize for being loud, for being powerful, for being her. And that is what self-love truly looks like—standing tall, unapologetic, and unafraid to take up the space you deserve. As women, we've been taught to shrink, to make ourselves smaller so that others feel more comfortable. But Maya Angelou? She said, "No more." She knew that her presence was a gift, and so she embraced it fully. She didn't hold back, and neither should you. Self-love is about honoring who you are, without hesitation. It's about walking into a room and saying, "I belong here," no matter how much the world tries to make you doubt it.

Perhaps the most important lesson Maya Angelou teaches us is the power of self-worth. Maya knew that her value didn't come from the approval of others, from fame, or from external success. Her worth came from within, from the deep understanding that she was enough, exactly as she was. Maya didn't let anyone or anything diminish her belief in herself, even in the face of hardship.

Maya's life wasn't about pretending she had it all together—it was about understanding that she was worthy, even in her darkest moments. She didn't need anyone's permission to stand in her truth. She made the choice every day to love herself, to forgive herself, and to be proud of who she was becoming. Self-love is an active practice. It's about looking at yourself in the mirror every single day and knowing that, no matter what mistakes you've made, no matter what obstacles you've faced, you are worthy of love, respect, and success. It's about choosing to rise again, even when you've been knocked down.

What Maya Angelou's life shows us is that self-love isn't a destination—it's a journey. A messy, complicated, beautiful journey. But in the end, it's the only thing that will set you free. Maya Angelou lived her truth unapologetically, and in doing so, she left a legacy that continues to inspire millions. She didn't just find success; she found herself. And that's the most powerful thing any of us can do.

Maya teaches us that we are not defined by our circumstances, our trauma, or our mistakes. We are defined by how we choose to love ourselves, how we choose to heal, and how we choose to stand tall in our worth. Her journey to self-love was long, but it was also transformative, not just for her, but for the entire world.

So, let's take a page from Maya's book. Let's choose ourselves. Let's choose to trust in our strength, to trust in our worth, and to trust that we are capable of far more than we can even imagine. Maya Angelou didn't just change the world with her words; she changed the world with her self-love. And so can you.

What Maya Angelou proves is that no matter where you start, no matter how hard the road may seem, you can always choose to rise. You can always choose to reclaim your power, to speak your truth, and to walk in your worth. Because, just like Maya, you are worthy of love, of success, and of the kind of life that makes you feel fully alive.

"You can't be afraid to fail. You can't be afraid to be yourself, to be imperfect, because that's where the magic happens."

Mindy Kaling

Final Words

So, here we are. You've made it through the pages of this book, and if you've been with me up to this point, I hope you've found more than just advice—you've found the beginning of something transformative. A shift, maybe, or even a lightbulb moment that clicked. But here's the truth: this is just the start. What you've learned here isn't a one-time fix or a magic formula that will suddenly make everything in your life perfect. No, it's a journey, a commitment. And while it won't always be easy (because life rarely is), the more you show up for yourself, the more you'll begin to notice the shifts. The moments when you choose your peace over drama, when you enforce your boundaries with love, when you say "no" without guilt, and when you lean into your power unapologetically.

This is where you get to decide how the next chapter of your life goes. You can keep doing the same old things, going through the motions, or you can take this newfound wisdom and let it fuel your transformation. The life you've always wanted, the life that's waiting for you on the other side of fear and self-doubt? It's within your reach.

And I'll tell you this—there's no better time than right now. You don't need to wait for the perfect moment, or for the stars to align. You've got everything inside you to step into your own power. You are worthy. You are enough. And it's time to stop looking for permission to shine.

When you choose self-love, you choose a life of abundance, joy, and strength. You choose to stop being a passive observer in your own story and instead become the active, bold author. No more shrinking, no more apologizing for your needs, and no more pretending you're anything less than the incredible, resilient woman you are.

So, from this moment on, let this be your reminder: You are the creator of your life. Every choice you make, every boundary you set, every action you take, is a reflection of your worth and your power. Embrace it.

I'll leave you with this: You've always had everything you needed to succeed—love, strength, resilience—inside you. Now it's time to claim it. The world is waiting for you to show up fully. Step into your power, unapologetically and fearlessly. Here's to living life on your terms.

With love,
Talia James

www.ingramcontent.com/pod-product-compliance
Lightning Source LLC
Chambersburg PA
CBHW061047250726
48653CB00001B/299